Thank God Its Thursday

ENCOUNTERING JESUS AT THE LORD'S TABLE
AS IF FOR THE LAST TIME

WILLIAM H. WILLIMON

Abingdon Press
Nashville

THANK GOD IT'S THURSDAY
ENCOUNTERING JESUS AT THE LORD'S TABLE AS IF FOR THE LAST TIME

Copyright © 2013 by Abingdon Press

All rights reserved.

This book is printed on acid-free paper.

Library of Congress Cataloging-in-Publication Data

Willimon, William H.
   Thank God it's Thursday : encountering Jesus at the Lord's table / William H. Willimon.
      p.   cm.
   ISBN 978-1-4267-4337-5 (pbk. : alk. paper) 1. Lord's Supper—Biblical teaching.
2. Bible. N.T. John—Criticism, interpretation, etc. I. Title.
   BS2615.6.L58W55 2013
   226.5′06—dc23

              2012038357

13 14 15 16 17 18 19 20 21 22—10 9 8 7 6 5 4 3 2 1

MANUFACTURED IN THE UNITED STATES OF AMERICA

CONTENTS

INTRODUCTION

And during supper Jesus...
—John 13:2

It's odd, even for the odd Gospel of John. Jesus is in Bethany, entertained by his good friends Mary and Martha (John 12:1-11). John casually remarks that Lazarus, whom Jesus has just raised from the dead, is there at the table. Lazarus whom he has just *raised from the dead?* Are you kidding?

Imagine being seated at that dinner table: "You know our rabbi, Jesus, don't you? And seated next to him is our brother Lazarus, who died last week. Thanks to Jesus, he's back among the living. No telltale grave stench, even. Please make yourself comfortable between them."

Settling uneasily in your seat, just being polite, you ask the table companion on your right, "Had a good week?"

Your fellow dinner guest replies, "Well, I was sick unto death, my sisters were frantic with worry, then I died, was entombed for three days, wrapped like a mummy. Jesus graciously stopped by the cemetery, shouted, 'Lazarus, come

V

out!' and raised me from the dead just in time for my sisters' dinner party. How was your week?"

The guest to your left, the young rabbi, says, "Unfortunately, no sooner had I raised Lazarus than my enemies vowed to kill me. I give myself no more than a week before they succeed."

Where are we? Welcome to the wonderfully weird world of the Gospel of John and to the holiest week of the church's year. And welcome to the truth about what God in Jesus Christ is up to in the world. God isn't just good and great; God is on the move toward us. Jesus joins us at the table, and whenever Jesus shows up, hold on to your hat; corpses rise from the dead, and we are shocked that God is more active than we imagined. The predictable, dull world is rendered strange, and even at a meal, Jesus, though unarmed, is extremely dangerous.

In intensifying his whole ministry at a meal, Jesus leads us into a world that is thick with subtle, secret meaning. A meal in which a piece of bread is called "my body broken for you," a cup of wine designated as "my blood shed for you," is almost too rich a metaphorical feast. We can spend a lifetime attempting to plumb the depths of such a mystery and never exhaust, much less consume, the meaning. This book on Maundy Thursday's mysteries is meant to increase enjoyment of this holy mystery rather merely to explain it.

One of my earliest writing ventures was *Sunday Dinner: The Lord's Supper and the Christian Life*,[1] a book that still strikes a chord in the eucharistic heart of the church. *Sunday Dinner* was my effort, as a young professor of liturgical theology at Duke, to demonstrate why few moments with Jesus are more significant than when he looks across the table and says, "Have some bread. Take some wine."

This present effort is a play on my book *Thank God It's Friday: Encountering the Seven Last Words from the Cross.*[2] My editor, Kathy Armistead, noting the church's gracious reception of that book, gave me the idea for this one.

Although I could have based these thoughts on any of the Gospels, I decided to work primarily with the Gospel of John, in which much of the last half of the Gospel takes place during a meal in a room in Jerusalem just before Passover. The liturgy of the church generally lets Luke, Matthew, or Mark handle Holy Week through Maundy Thursday and then turns to John for Good Friday and the Passion. I propose to allow John to teach us on Thursday.

In four long chapters (John 13:1–16:33) the Word-made-flesh, God-with-us turns away from instruction of the world to host a farewell supper with his disciples, during which he tells them how to live once he is physically absent from them.

John's Gospel is rich—almost too rich—for the interpreter. To get one's good news from the fourth Gospel is willingly to enter a luxuriant figurative world in which few things are as they first appear. Our world has been made strange by the advent of a God whom almost nobody expected. In heaps of symbols, metaphors, similes, and images, John teaches us how to read the world as Christians, gradually, sign by sign, leading us into a reality we might have missed without John's words.

Augustine described his own conversion to Christ as a long process of learning how to read the Bible. His teacher, Ambrose, helped Augustine see that in the odd, thick, mysterious world of scripture, *bread* means more than what you had for dinner, *fish* is more than fish, and things like vines, water, women, and men on crosses are almost never as they first appear.

I have had to learn to love the Gospel of John and the way it refuses to be managed by my intellect. Jesus, as John recalls him, reminds you of the Jesus we meet in the Synoptics—Matthew, Mark, and Luke—but this is Jesus as Christ taken up to the nth degree. Somehow John's Jesus manages to be both strange and remote and also intimate and close at hand. I have found Jesus to be, paradoxically, no more distant from us and no nearer to us than when he is at table with us.

The Gospel that begins with, "And the Word became flesh and lived among us, and we have seen his glory" (John 1:14), is a supremely eucharistic, table-talk Gospel in which Jesus saves some of his best stuff until the end when he settles down at the dinner table with his twelve best friends (who are also his worst betrayers) and unpacks his significance for them, having a bite to eat with them just before he is tortured to death for them.

God's incarnation, Jesus' act of redemption, our grand reconciliation—all these weighty, true, but unfathomable mysteries are on the table on Thursday. The Lord's Supper is always a demonstration of God with us: none other than the great, glorious God present with none other than the lousiest sinners. If you can't be safe from God at a carnal, mundane, fleshly, ordinary gathering of friends around the supper table, well, where can you hide?

Will Willimon

Maundy Thursday

Notes

1. William H. Willimon, *Sunday Dinner: The Lord's Supper and the Christian Life* (Nashville: Upper Room, 1981).

2. William H. Willimon, *Thank God It's Friday: Encountering the Seven Last Words from the Cross* (Nashville: Abingdon Press, 2006).

Lord Jesus Christ, three times a day you reveal to us that our lives are sustained by the gifts of others, strangers whose names we will never know. Someone tilled the soil and planted the seed, harvested the wheat, stored the grain, and then shipped it across the continent, labored before the break of day to bake the bread and deliver it to the store. Some of these strangers toiled long hours, or had their bodies broken, or were paid poorly so that we might, without much effort on our part, break bread today.

By your Holy Spirit remind us how much we owe to you and to those who make our lives possible through their sacrifice. You bless us by the gifts of others. Because we can't thank them all for making this meal possible, we pause to thank you for all of them and for all their gifts. Amen.

CHAPTER I

UNCOMFORTABLE SUPPER

*Now before the festival of the Passover, Jesus knew that his hour had come
to depart from this world and go to the Father. Having loved his own
who were in the world, he loved them to the end. The devil had already
put it into the heart of Judas son of Simon Iscariot to betray him. And
during supper Jesus, knowing that the Father had given all things into
his hands, and that he had come from God and was going to God, got up
from the table, took off his outer robe, and tied a towel around himself.
Then he poured water into a basin and began to wash the disciples' feet
and to wipe them with the towel that was tied around him.*
—John 13:1-5

We owe to the Jews our custom of saying "grace"
before we eat. Israel worships at the Temple,
the synagogue, and even at the family din-
ner table. To pray before engaging in ingestion is to claim
eating and drinking—thoroughly necessary, utterly human

activities—as acts full of divine signification. To pray the simple "God is great, God is good, let us thank him for our food" is to say a great deal about God and about food as a gift of God.

Many of us Methodists like to follow the Wesleys in praying, "Be present at our table, Lord, be here and everywhere adored." To invoke God's presence, asking God to come to the table, opens the simple act of sharing food and soothing our hunger to even greater meaning. We hunger for more than food, thirst for more than water. Thus, each of the sections of this book about Maundy Thursday's meal opens with a table blessing. I'm sure John would have me add that any time you say a prayer at the table, any table, hold on to your hats. Something about the Trinity loves to show up at dinnertime.

How typical of Jesus to save his whole point, his grandest moments of revelation, for the dinner table. When we hear the word *Incarnation*, we tend to think of Jesus' birth, the true meaning of Christmas—the Eternal Word became flesh and moved in with us. And yet, Maundy Thursday is a reminder that the Incarnation is more than the birth of Jesus; the Incarnation is also the whole life, death, and resurrection of Jesus; everything Jesus did with us and was to us; and his speaking and acting and especially his eating. He met us on our own turf, coming to our workaday world in which there are hungers to be assuaged, food to be prepared, dishes to be washed, and guests to be invited; and although some of us gorge on too much, others are sent away from the table sorrowful and empty. Maundy Thursday is an affirmation of the everydayness of our God: God in the present tense and a God who refused and even now continues to refuse to leave us be, especially at dinnertime.

You already know that no meal is merely ingestion. The table is a place where the consumption of food is miraculously transformed into occasion for conviviality, conversation and revelation, communion and reunion. At table, mundane bodily function is given spiritual significance. Mealtimes tend to be life's highlights. The family meal, even breakfast, becomes a kind of sacrament of family life, an outward and visible sign of an inward and spiritual grace. In every meal, there is always more, and the more is that which makes life worth living.

What you may yet discover is that in every meal with Jesus, there is even more of more. The augmented significance that Jesus always brings to the table tends to be at the heart of the Christian faith.

I hope that you find reassurance that, if you want to commune deeply with God, you need not climb some high mountain (like Moses when receiving the Ten Commandments) or journey out into the wilderness (like the Israelites during the Exodus). You simply must pray a prayer of blessing—say grace—at your breakfast table. God will do the rest.

Unlike the Synoptic Gospels that portray Jesus presiding over the Passover Seder, John says that Jesus' climactic meal occurred before the Passover. Jesus saves his best teaching, not for a sermon in the synagogue or inside the Temple at a high-ritual moment, but rather for an evening meal among friends.

His hour had come to depart from this world and go to the Father.
—John 13:1

We awaited this hour throughout the Gospel of John. Some of us thought that his hour would be an hour of grandeur, a high moment when Jesus would at last throw off his humble humanity and begin to act like the Messiah we wanted him to be. But no, his hour will not be a triumphal march into Jerusalem, during which he seizes power, takes over the government, and kicks out the Romans. His hour will be spent with friends around the dinner table, patiently giving us the core of his teaching.

John says that Jesus' "last supper" was on the eve of the celebration of Passover, which is Israel's celebration of independence from slavery. Jews know by heart the great prayer, "Hear O Israel, the LORD is our God, the LORD alone (Deut. 6:4). God's people are not free to bow before other lords and lordlets, even one so ruthlessly presumptive as Caesar. How bitterly ironic that on Passover, Israel's grand day of independence from slavery, some of God's cherished people collaborate with pagan Caesar to put to death God's Son. When all Jerusalem celebrates the actual feast, Jesus will be lying in the tomb (John 19:38-42), and Caesar's gods will think they are victorious.

Jesus had spoken rather ominously of "his hour" (John

2:24; 7:30; 8:20). "His hour" is a decisive moment. Here at the table we are told that at last his hour has come. Luke speaks of Jesus' death as a kind of exodus (Luke 9:31), clearly evoking Passover and deliverance. John calls his hour a departure (*metabaino*, a "cross over," John 13:1). In John, Jesus is crossing from this world to another, making a crossing before us, returning to where he had come before the Incarnation (John 1:1-5, 14). When someone dies, we say that person has "passed away." Jesus is passing over. Thus John gives heightened meaning to *Passover*. Jesus is passing over not just from slavery to freedom but also from death to life, passing over from this world to another.

And yet, here at table with his friends, in celebrating a meal, the most social and communal of human acts, Jesus shows that he has no intention of crossing over alone; he will, in some sense, take us with him. As he lifts the cup and passes the bread, he is leading us to a place we would not have—could not have—gone without his taking us there.

Descent and Assent

At this table, on this night, we are at a turning point from the incarnate Jesus' ministry here among us. He begins a crossover through his death to resurrection and future life with us in the community of love. The one who descended to us from the realm of light and life (John 1:1, 9; 3:13) is preparing to ascend to the Father who sent him. In him, heaven has done business with earth; now in him earth shall be exalted heavenward. The Son of God, the Eternal Logos,

5

the One who was with God at the beginning, the One who is God, strips for work and kneels before us.

And during supper Jesus, knowing that the Father had given all things into his hands, and that he had come from God and was going to God, got up from the table, took off his outer robe, and tied a towel around himself.

—*John 13:2-4*

On another night, ancestor Jacob had seen in a dream a great ladder let down from heaven with angels ascending and descending (Gen. 28). Tonight is the eve of "the hour" when there is once again heaven-to-earth traffic. Something about the Father refuses to be confined to heaven, God in heaven alone. God so loved the world that God gave God's Son for the world (John 3:16). The Son descends in order to reclaim a world in the grip of night; soon the Son will ascend in order to bring the whole world back to the God of Light.

C. S. Lewis depicts Christ's ascent and descent as an image of all that Christ did and said:

> In the Christian story God descends to reascend. He comes down; down from the heights of absolute being into time and space, down into humanity....But He goes down to come up again and bring the whole ruined world up with Him....One may think of a diver, first reducing himself to nakedness, then glancing in mid-air, then gone with a splash, vanished, rushing down through green and warm water in black and cold water, down through increasing pressure into the death-like region of ooze and slime and old decay; then up again, back to

colour and light, his lungs almost bursting, till suddenly
he breaks surface again, holding in his hand the dripping,
precious thing that he went down to recover.[1]

This is the dramatic, paradoxical tension that John sus-
tains throughout his Gospel: the divine has become human.
Eternity has entered time. And when God shows up as the
Word Made Flesh, at table or anywhere else, be prepared to
have your boundaries of the human and the divine, of eternity and time, shattered.

We couldn't come to God, so God came to us, meeting
us where we live, in the most mundane of locations—at the
dinner table. Because our attempts at righteousness always
went bad, Christ climbs down to the unrighteous (2 Cor.
5:21) then ascends a bloody cross, not only demonstrating
the depths of our evil but also plumbing the unfathomable
depths of God's love. And because God elected to be God for
us, God with us, God in Christ could not return to God the
Father without bringing us along, offering back to the Father
the whole, beloved, yet deeply forlorn and lost human race.

Beginning with the Deed

Sometimes, while reading John's Gospel, my eyes blear
and everything fades into a vague misty blue. The Fourth
Gospel can have that effect on people. John's Gospel is
packed with many high-sounding, spiritual words that tend
to float upward. Some tire of John's long, religious-sounding
speeches. I loved the Canadian film *The Gospel of John*, in

which the Fourth Gospel is vividly rendered word for word in some stunning scenes. But it takes the film over three hours to do it. A friend who watched this movie said that he grumbled in frustration toward the end (surely in one of those long, redundant discourses in the last half of the Gospel), "Will Jesus ever shut up?"

But note that once we get to the table, after a rather intricate, thick theological introduction in John 13:1, words are laid aside and things unfold through haunting gestures done in silence: "during supper Jesus...got up...took off...tied a towel...poured water...began to wash...and to wipe."

You see every move in your mind. Not a word is spoken; it's all in the action.

> And during supper Jesus, knowing that the Father had given all things into his hands, and that he had come from God and was going to God, got up from the table, took off his outer robe, and tied a towel around himself. Then he poured water into a basin and began to wash the disciples' feet and to wipe them with the towel that was tied around him.

Some years ago, the errant Jesus Seminar made much mischief in their voting on which words, if any, Jesus actually spoke. Not many, said the voters in the seminar. Who told the Jesus Seminar that Christians worship the words of Jesus? We worship Jesus as the Word Incarnate, which means that we are attentive not only to what Jesus says but also to what he does. In Jesus, the Word Made Flesh became the Word as

Deed. Having said, down through the ages, "I love you," God turned love into action and showed up as the Son (Heb. 1:2).

How sad that many of us are conditioned to think that when we go to church to be present with Jesus we are supposed to sit and listen to words. In many so-called contemporary services, the congregation doesn't even sing, because of unsingable songs, as would-be communal Christian worship degenerates into a spectator sport in which the passive many watch the performing few at worship.

I therefore think there are few things more important than the restoration of the Lord's Supper as an every-Sunday activity for every congregation. Let's remind ourselves that we Protestants who attempt noneucharistic worship on the majority of Sundays are decidedly in a minority of the world's Christians. At table (at least as the Synoptic Gospels—Matthew, Mark, and Luke—tell it), Jesus clearly said, "*Do* this," not think about, meditate upon, or have deep feelings for this. In going against centuries of church practice and the majority of Christians at worship today, we not only in effect have excommunicated millions of God's people from the Lord's Table but also have given many the false impression that we would rather talk about Jesus than to be present with Jesus, and that following Jesus is a matter of what we think or feel rather than what we do.

"So if I, your Lord and Teacher, have washed your feet, you also ought to wash one another's feet. For I have set you an example, that you also should do as I have done to you. Very truly, I tell you, servants are not

greater than their master, nor are messengers greater than the one who sent them. If you know these things, you are blessed if you do them."
—*John 13:14-17*

In John, Jesus is big on words. But tonight, at the table, he doesn't only say the good news; he shows us as he enacts his gospel, embodies his sermons with basin and towel, simply and directly commanding us to do the same. In other Gospels, Jesus tells some memorable parables; tonight he performs parabolically by kneeling at his disciples' feet and enacting the gospel.

When Peter breaks the silence by blurting out his surprise that Jesus would act like a slave (yes, the actual Greek word is *slave* rather than the softer *servant*), Jesus responds (in John 13:6-11) with an enigmatic explanation alluding to the Lamb of God and the metaphor of washing. Peter is horrified to see his Lord on his knees before him, washing Peter's dirty feet, and responds in much the same way as he rebuked Jesus in his first prediction of his death and suffering in Mark 8:32.

Jesus answers with a more detailed explication of his foot washing, concluding with, "If you know these things, you are blessed if you *do* them" (John 13:17, italics mine). Yes, that's often just the problem, isn't it? We know, but we fail to act upon our knowledge. The challenge with faith is not only knowing about Jesus but also doing as Jesus.

Many modern people complain that their problem with Jesus is that they lack sufficient knowledge about Jesus. There are so many gaps in our information about him, and some of the information—say when one compares the story of Jesus in Mark with that told in John—seems ambiguous and conflicting. I suspect that Jesus is easier to handle if we turn him into an intellectual problem. We await the results of more historical research on Jesus. We assume that if we just had more verifiable, uncontested facts about Jesus, we would know for sure about Jesus.

The modern world was, in great part, an intellectual quest for sure and certain knowledge. History became a science as scholars methodically peeled away the accumulated layers of myth and fanciful, credulous fables and dug down to the absolutely certain facts. Dare to think!

I remind you that Jesus never said, "Think about me." It was always, "Follow me." Or more typical of John's Gospel, Jesus says even more engagingly, "Love me." Love that is only knowledge of love is not yet true love. As Jesus says, it's blessed to know him, but more blessed is to do as he does (John 13:17), transforming his enigmatic action at the table into an example for us to follow throughout life, a command for us to obey.

Sometimes we preachers unwittingly imply that the greatest challenge of the Christian faith is in right thinking. Jesus is presented as a sort of folk philosopher who is tough to understand without the explication of a preacher. The Christian faith is a set of sometimes-challenging, frequently baffling ideas or principles. The sermon begins, "Three biblical principles for a more fulfilling life are..." or, "Now I will attempt to explain confusing Jesus to you."

The intellectual love of the faith is indeed a blessed thing. We are enjoined to grow in our knowledge of the Lord; indeed, I hope this book will help you do just that. Yet even more blessed is active following of the faith—not thinking but doing the faith.

Preaching Presence

Still, John's Gospel is best thought of as a sermon. Try reducing the Gospels to biography, or merely to a report on history, and they will come across as botched, boring history. John doesn't just want to inform you about the past facts of Jesus; John wants to convert you into present faith in Jesus so that you will be enticed to follow Jesus.

Among the lessons that I as a preacher learn from preacher John is that my job as a preacher is not to dumb Jesus down. How many times have I as a preacher read aloud to the congregation some biblical text and watched listeners squirm. Then I begin my sermon, in effect, "Settle down. I can see that Jesus has made you confused and uncomfortable. Well, here is what Jesus was trying to say if he, like me, had the benefit of a seminary education."

I thus imply that, after my skilled explanation of Jesus, you will cease to be bothered by Jesus. Rather than encounter Jesus, you simply repeat what you have always thought about Jesus before you really met him. You can go home having had some sort of vague spiritual experience rather than being challenged by the living, demandingly present Christ.

Rather than attempt to explain Jesus, John presents him in all of his wondrous mysteriousness. Rather than close the gap between you and Jesus, John opens up the gap so that, once you see John's Jesus in action at the table with his disciples, you say, "I guess I didn't know Jesus as well as I first thought."

We don't preach about Jesus; we preach Jesus. In the sermon, I'm not going to work on Jesus as an intellectual problem, but rather I am going to allow Jesus to use the sermon to work on you through his stunning, challenging, real presence. What you most want is not a set of simple ideas about Jesus; you want Jesus. Thus the martyr Dietrich Bonhoeffer said that the purpose of a sermon is to allow the risen Christ to walk among his people.

I tell you, looking out from the pulpit while I preach, some Sundays I can almost see Christ roaming the aisles, often stopping unexpectedly at pews where innocent persons are listening passively, tapping them on the shoulder or whopping them upside the head, enlisting them, calling them by name into his service, transforming a sermon from harmless information into risky vocation.

As a Christian communicator, I marvel at John's willingness to let mysterious Jesus stay a mystery, to present Christ in a way that frustrates simple explication. John's masterful, strange narration of, say, the story of Nicodemus coming to Jesus by night (John 3) is so much better even than my very best attempts to explain to you what John meant by his story of Nicodemus coming to Jesus.

In John, Jesus is the Word, the eternal *Logos*, a loaded Greek word that can mean not only "word" but also "reason." So the reason for John's Gospel—the rationale for telling the story of Jesus at the table this night with his disciples or the point, if you will—is not some idea about Jesus; it is Jesus.

We frequently say that we "prepare a meal." Jesus uses a meal to prepare his people for their more lasting home, for his departure as he returns to the Father, and more to his exemplary point, for their work here and now in the world by being an example for them—with basin and towel.

These actions at the table are preparation. The table is not their final destination. That's a good thing for us to remember any time two or three or more of us are gathered for worship. Something within each of us would love to snuggle close to Jesus at this table, there to linger with him forever in the serenity and conviviality of the meal. But when you are at table with Jesus, worshiping him, adoring his presence, you do so only to "rise, let us be on our way" (John 14:31). He nourishes us at the table in order to strengthen us to walk perilous paths in the night beyond the table. He gathers us in church in worship in order to disperse us in service into the world. So we gather here in the warm camaraderie of the table on Thursday to send Jesus off into another world, only to have him end the supper by sending us out in service to this world.

Jesus Getting Down and Dirty

Feet are literally the lowest, earthiest part of the body. "To put under the feet" was a humiliating gesture of the victor over the vanquished (Ps. 8:6). In the ancient world, feet got dirty on dusty roads (Mark 6:11). Washing a guest's feet was an act of highest hospitality (Gen. 18:4; Luke 7:44). Moses removed his shoes in a holy place in order not to defile it (Exod. 3:5). To "fall at the feet" of someone is an act of humility and self-abasement (1 Sam. 25:24; Mark 5:22).[2] Just a few days before Maundy Thursday, Mary anointed Jesus' feet (John 12:1-8).

It's a touching gesture, the washing of feet. It's nice to see the pope kneel and wash the feet of a young priest on Maundy Thursday at the Vatican.[3] But when Jesus arrives at the feet of Judas, I react with revulsion. Amid all of Jesus' high-sounding and loving words at the table, I almost forgot. At the table with the Twelve was Judas, who, a short time from now, will, by a kiss, send Jesus off to a diabolical death.

In scripture, vanquished enemies are put under the victors' feet (Josh. 10:24; Mal. 4:3). Here at table, Jesus does a shocking reversal, placing himself under the feet of his worst enemy who also happens to be one of his good friends.

How much easier this gesture would have been if it had been offered to the rest of the Twelve but not to Judas, if Jesus had drawn the line between the passive acquiescence with evil of the Eleven and the active betrayal of Judas. At least the others got not a dime from their betrayal of their master. We wish that Jesus had waited until Judas made his exit before Jesus knelt and washed his disciples' feet.

No, there's Jesus tenderly caressing the feet of Judas as

if he were the Beloved Disciple at Jesus' bosom. Judas will shortly use those same feet to walk from the meal to sell out his Savior. Is the foot-washing John's version of Jesus' abrasive command to love our enemies and to pray for those who persecute us (Matt. 5:44)? Or is it John's way of having Jesus say, as he says elsewhere, "I've come to seek and to save the lost"? How much easier for the remaining Eleven, if Jesus had not given his life (only) for sinners and if he had not stooped down and lovingly washed the feet of Judas Iscariot.

When the Alabama legislature passed a law that penalized our citizens for giving aid, comfort, food, housing, jobs, or transportation to undocumented immigrants, many churches of Alabama knew that the immigration law was an attack upon our Christ-assigned work.

I argued with the governor (who was a retired Methodist pastor turned politician who shamelessly defended the law), "Unfortunately, Jesus doesn't allow his people to choose between the deserving and the undeserving poor, the documented and the undocumented homeless and hungry. He commands us actively to love all those in need."

Some legislators replied, "But these people are *illegal.* The church shouldn't be aiding and abetting lawbreakers."

Hey, before Jesus Christ, so far as our relationship to God was concerned, we were all illegal! His New Covenant, given at table, documented a bunch of illicit sinners as God's beloved. At the time I was duking it out with our right-wing, ill-advised governor, I didn't think about this Judas-foot-washing episode from John 13, but I wish I had. If Jesus had reason to wash Judas's feet, in effect aiding and abetting his own murderer, harboring the worst of criminals at his own table, well, he'll wash anybody's feet—even mine, even the governor's, even yours, no matter where your dirty feet have taken you.

Judas receives more attention than any other person in the story except Jesus (in John 13:1-30). Is this a warning to contemporary disciples? Thus that great Catholic apologist for the faith, G. K. Chesterton, dared to call Judas the very first Christian: "Judas Iscariot was one of the very earliest of all possible early Christians. And the whole point about him was that his hand was in the same dish; the traitor is always a friend, or he could never be a foe."[4] Sorry, if your idea of "Christian" is someone who has overcome the problem of sin and now sits at Jesus' table with clean hands and a spotless conscience. Watch Jesus wash Judas's feet and repeat after me: *Jesus Christ came to seek and to save sinners, only sinners.*

If Judas can be thought of as the first Christian, then that also makes this supper our earliest glimpse of the church.

The church is made up of those sinners who have responded to Jesus' offer to be washed from head to toe and then regularly to sup with Jesus into eternity. That's as much as the church can claim. As Bonhoeffer wrote:

> God goes to all people in their need,
> fills body and spirit with God's bread,
> goes for Christians and heathens to Calvary's death,
> and forgives them both.[5]

Who is a Christian? A sinner who has been washed head to toe by Jesus.

What is the church? A ragtag group of betrayers who are regularly served and nourished by Jesus.

Presumably Satan didn't need to trouble the hearts of the other disciples to incite them to betrayal; among us, unfaithfulness to Jesus comes quite naturally.

"Were you there when they crucified my Lord?" we sing. Each of us knows the answer. We meet no sin among the enemies of Jesus that we disciples do not first encounter in our own hearts.

And yet (here is the good news), with whom does Jesus choose to spend his last meal, whose feet does he wash, to whom does he offer himself and this meal? To betrayers— that is, *all of us.*

Jesus is on his way to glory, but he will not be glorified alone, insisting on one last meal, one final night of conviviality with his most beloved friends, who also happen to be his most sinful betrayers.

You'd have to be a disciple of Jesus to know why we call this glorious good news.

Loving as God Loves

I'm sure that Jesus' loving, servile gesture felt like a slap in the face to Judas as the grand betrayer prepared to go forth and sell out his Lord and Savior. Jesus' act of humility had to be humiliating to Judas. If so, John says nothing about it.

I wish the story ended with Judas seeing Jesus kneel before him, washing his feet, finally coming to his senses, and saying, "Wait a minute! I'm crazy to betray my loving Lord and my own true self by this evil deed."

As you know, the story didn't end that way. Even after Jesus' loving act, Judas went right ahead and acted publicly as he had secretly conceived in his mind to do. That's true for most of us. I wish I could say that, when someone has forgiven me for my act of injustice against him or her, I am transformed by his or her charity and say, "Wait a minute! I was really, really wrong to do what I did to you. I'm so, so sorry."

In Matthew's Gospel (5:39), Jesus does not commend turning the other cheek, going the second mile, forgiving someone seventy-times-seven times, because it's sure to bring out the best in perpetrators, sure to help them see the error of their ways. Nor does Jesus commend washing the feet of a defector and deserter like Judas in order to transform him into the Beloved Disciple.

Jesus washes his disciples' feet, including the feet of Judas, because that's the way things are now that he has revealed the truth about God. Jesus is going to prepare a place for his sinful disciples, a place where what he does this night around the table will be done in eternity, and, wherever Jesus is, that's the place where we can be with him. He gives them an example of how they ought to behave so that they can be fortunate enough to be on the way, following his way, to where he is going.

A woman in my church heard my sermon on forgiveness and took it to heart, directly applying it to a situation in her work. Her boss had done wrong against her. She had tried to confront him with the error of what he had done but had failed. Spurred on to righteousness by my sermon on forgiveness, she went to him and said, "I want you to know that I forgive you. I don't condone what you have done, and I may never forget what you have done, but as a Christian I feel compelled to forgive you."

The next day, she was fired. If she forgave hoping that it would finally bring her boss to his senses and he would be remorseful, she failed. If she forgave because she felt compelled to do so because she had learned the truth about reality—Jesus Christ—then I see her not only as an exemplary Christian but also as a grand example that Jesus not only commands us to "Go thou and do likewise" but also gives us, even us, the miraculous grace to do what he commands.

"Do you understand what I do?" (John 13:12), Jesus has the nerve to ask us.

"Well, not really," we think in our hearts. Such boundary-breaking, risky, total love will always be for us an incomprehensible mystery. Fortunately, we need not fully understand it; we just have to do it.

"Watch me now," he seems to say as he kneels, lit only

by the flickering lights on the supper table. "Watch. Here's how you do the discipleship thing. Here's how to get really close to the true and living God. Watch. All you have to do is take a dirty, smelly foot of an outrageous criminal like Judas, hold it tenderly in your hand, and wash it as if you were caressing the hand of your most beloved friend. See? Is that so difficult?"

Notes

1. C. S. Lewis, *Miracles* (London: Collins, 1960 [1947]), 115–16.

2. Because of the lowly status, feet became an infrequent biblical metaphor for male sexual organs, but I won't trouble you with those references.

3. In 2006, Pope Benedict began washing the feet of a dozen laymen at Maundy Thursday services.

4. G. K. Chesterton, *The New Jerusalem* (London: Hodder and Stoughton), 286.

5. Tom Greggs, *Theology Against Religion: Constructive Dialogues with Bonhoeffer and Barth* (London: T. & T. Clark, 2011), 110.

Lord, make me a person I couldn't be without your gracious intervention into my life.

I gobble down food without a thought of its significance. Slow me down; make me sit still.

I want what I want now. Give me patience by reading the long Gospel of John.

I eat on the run. Teach me the grace of doing nothing. Even in church.

Teach me good manners and consideration for others at the table. Make me treat this gaggle of fellow sinners as if they were brothers and sisters, baptized into this crazy quilt called church.

Preach. Talk to me in public. Say things to me that I dare not say to myself. Embarrass me in front of friends. Make me different.

Particularly in church. Amen.

CHAPTER

II

MAKING AN EXAMPLE OF JESUS

"So if I, your Lord and Teacher, have washed your feet, you also ought to wash one another's feet. For I have set you an example, that you also should do as I have done to you. Very truly, I tell you, servants are not greater than their master, nor are messengers greater than the one who sent them. If you know these things, you are blessed if you do them."
—John 13:14-17

Why does John have no account of the so-called institution of the Lord's Supper? The core words of the meal—"this is my body" and "this is my blood"—presaging his sacrifice upon the cross, go unmentioned by John. Of course, John's Gospel is the most "sacramental" of gospels in which commonplace eating and drinking, food and sacrifice, and bathing and water have mysterious, God-infused meaning, which is the very essence of sacrament.

I'm sure that when Jesus spoke about washing and Peter pled for a total body wash, everybody at table thought "baptism." And when Jesus knelt down at his disciples' feet and washed them, I'm sure that everyone eventually knew that action was meant as interpretation of his descent even to death on a cross.

In John, Jesus switches from the Synoptic Gospels' "do this" in bread and wine to "do this" with basin and towel. Whereas the other Gospels focus upon the memorial of Jesus in bread and wine, John focuses upon the baptismal-like deed of washing feet and Jesus' command to continue to perform such service in the future (13:15). In other words, John subtly turns our attention from what Jesus does to what we are to do.

Even more difficult for the disciples (us), Jesus not only washes Judas's feet, not only washes all of his disciples' feet but also explicitly, directly commands them to copy him and to wash everybody else's feet!

It's almost as if Jesus knew we might later think, "Well, it's OK for Jesus to wash feet, to serve sinners, and to love the lost. After all, Jesus is the Son of God, the Word Made Flesh. As for us mortals, we are frail, limited folk who can't be expected to act like Jesus."

We wish.

Many people in my church believe that homosexuality is a great, serious sin. If that's true, then a question provoked by John 13 is: how many gay, lesbian, and transgendered sinners' feet have you recently washed?

Who would expect limited people like us, full of prejudice and sin, to copy Jesus, to try hard to mimic the Son of God? *Jesus*, that's who.

"So if I, your Lord and Teacher, have washed your feet, you also ought to wash one another's feet. For I have set you an example, that you also should do as I have done to you. Very truly, I tell you, servants are not greater than their master, nor are messengers greater than the one who sent them."
—*John 13:14-16*

How we wish Jesus had only taken up his cross and died for our sin, a divine robot born only in order to die for us, a savior for whom salvation meant only a washing away of our sins. Sadly—for our compromised and accommodated Christianity—Jesus told us that following him would result in a cross for us, too, a cross that we were to take up daily and drag after him, not only talking as he talked but also walking the way he walked.

Many have noted the odd way in which the Apostles' Creed tells the basics of Jesus by saying, "born of the virgin Mary, suffered under Pontius Pilate." All of Jesus' earthly deeds and words are covered in one comma? This is a truncated view not only of the significance of Jesus but also of the Christian life in the light of Jesus. Here in chapter 13, Jesus explicitly says that his deeds not only are of salvific significance but also are exemplary. We must not only believe what Jesus says but also do as he does.

I remember conducting a workshop on preaching for Mennonite pastors. I showed them a video of a sermon I preached on Jesus' Sermon on the Mount. Mennonites, like Wesleyans, are big on the Sermon on the Mount. In my sermon I skillfully, artistically (if I do say so) reframed the sermon as a poetic vision of the future, not a list of rules for the present. I spoke of how the sermon is eschatological, pointing to God's promised future.

After showing my sermon, I asked the gathered pastors what they thought of my creative homiletics. A young Mennonite pastor asked, "Did it ever occur to you to say, 'Just do it'?"

Just turn the other cheek? Just go the second mile? Just forgive enemies?

We have multiple means of avoiding Jesus' claim upon our lives. One way of evading Jesus is a poetic, creative sermon!

There are a couple of things to note about this matter of Jesus as an example to poor, struggling sinners such as we. First, I know that the notion that Jesus is not only our savior but also our example could be naive. American theologian Reinhold Niebuhr taught that it was unrealistic and simplistic for Christians to attempt to apply Jesus' "love" to modern social problems and political situations. "Justice," taught Niebuhr, was a more realistic goal than "love," which is personal, subjective, and unfit for application to complicated social matters. Therefore Niebuhr's "Christian Realism" said almost nothing about John's concern for loving fellow Christians in the church, focusing mostly on how

Christians might do justice in the United States. Niebuhr was much more concerned with responsibilities of citizens in a liberal democracy than with the behavior of Christians in the church.

John's Gospel was not beloved by Niebuhr (I'm not sure if any of the Gospels were loved by Niebuhr). John teaches that Jesus taught and demonstrated love, defined love in such a way as to make love the whole point, the greatest fruit of life in Christ. I expect that John would say that whether or not Jesus' command to love is realistic or not depends upon how you define reality. John begins his Gospel with clear allusion to Genesis 1 and the creation of the world: "In the beginning [Greek: *genesis*] was the Word." Get it? The advent of Jesus is almost like God started over and re-created the world as God intended the world to be. Jesus isn't just our precious Savior; he's a whole new world. Jesus is more than of merely personal significance; Christ is the truth about the whole point of the world. Jesus is not here just to give you a more purposeful life, a better reason to get out of bed in the morning, a sort of spiritual means for making America work; Jesus is here to show you the whole truth about reality. He is the fact of life all the way down.

I recall seeing the late Jerry Falwell being interviewed on TV. Falwell was asked about his enthusiastic support for the then-current Iraq war. He replied to the interviewer that the United States had been attacked, that something realistic must be done, that Saddam Hussein was no better than Hitler, that it was better to fight them in Iraq than in New

York, and so on. Then the interviewer asked something like, "But as a Christian, are you bothered that we are responding exclusively through military action?"

Falwell seemed a bit defensive, saying something like, "Well, Christian love is mainly for individuals, not for nations. Nations need to do what is realistic to preserve their freedom as a nation." In other words, Jesus is irrelevant, and the way he walked (and commanded us to walk) is silly.

We're all Niebuhrians now.

I wonder: if Falwell had lived to witness the sorry aftermath of our invasion and occupation of Iraq—the millions we have squandered in bogus "nation-building," the huge cost, and the paltry result—would he still think of the invasion of Iraq as "realistic"?

Second, I know that claiming Jesus as our example could be self-delusional. It can be dangerous for me to think I am a one-to-one direct embodiment of Jesus, simply doing as Jesus did. The WWJD—What would Jesus do?—approach to ethical reasoning was a short-lived phenomenon. For one thing, Jesus in the Gospels does not encounter or respond to every single ethical dilemma that we might face. For another thing, explaining my actions as "simply doing as Jesus did" might let me off the hook for not using my God-given brain, carefully discerning what is right in this circumstance.

And yet let's be honest: he said, "*Do* this." Let my actions at table be your example for life. It is a daunting thing for Jesus, in his active, suffering love, to turn from what he is doing and say to us, his disciples, "Watch me now. Do you see what I'm doing here? Now, you try it."

"Who, me? I'm just an ordinary guy attempting to get by as best I can. It's not like I'm a saint," I protest.

We thus dismiss Jesus' example as "too idealistic" or "unrealistic," which is fine if you are the Son of God, but not if you are an ordinary person like me.

Sorry. Jesus could not be more explicit as he kneels and washes the feet of his betrayers:

"For I have set you an example, that you also should do as I have done to you."
—John 13:15

How often Jesus used exemplary talk, "Follow me" (Matt. 9:9). First Peter 2:21 says that Christ left us an example, "that you should follow in his steps." Down through the ages, some of the faith's most distinguished practitioners have stressed Christ not only as our Savior who does for us what we cannot do for ourselves but also as our example who means for us to do as he does. What could be clearer than Jesus' statement that "whoever does not take up the cross and follow me is not worthy of me" (Matt. 10:38)?

Søren Kierkegaard, in his *Training in Christianity*,[1] says that Christ not only is located behind us to drive us on but also stands before us to beckon us on. Christ not only commands us to see him as an example but also blesses us by saying that he will give us what we need to be an example. Kierkegaard says that Christ came to call a group of

29

self-sacrificial followers and ended up with a gaggle of super-ficial, self-interested "admirers"![2]

Christian martyr to the Nazis, Dietrich Bonhoeffer, took Christ as an example with complete seriousness, even unto death. "Only he who believes is obedient and only he who is obedient believes," said Bonhoeffer, implying that it is impossible to claim to be a believer and then fail to be obedient, and also that we really grow in our ability to believe as we dare to obey.[3] Even as we stress Jesus as our ethical example, it's good to be reminded, by Bonhoeffer, that we are summoned to conform ourselves not only to Christ's acts but also to his person: "We are summoned to an exclusive attachment to His person."[4] Our affection for and attachment to the person of Christ is prior to and higher than even Christian ethics. Our ethics in the name of Christ is an outgrowth of our worship of Christ. Faith in Christ as Lord is prior to obedience to Christ as example. And in conforming to him as our example, we come to worship him more deeply as our Savior. He is a pattern for life, but he is more to us than just a pattern. He doesn't just show the way; he is the way. He is not only the way but also the truth and even the life (John 14:6).

Friends for Life

Jesus calls us not simply followers of his example. He dares to call us friends. The language is of relatedness and friendship, not formal codes and actions. We act in certain ways in obedience to Christ because he has related to us as our friend.

I suppose the most popular advocate of Jesus as an example was Charles Sheldon, a pastor from Topeka. Sheldon's *In His Steps* may be the most widely read religious book in history.[5] The book is full of high moral idealism in which a pastor publicly proclaims that he intends to move through life asking a deceptively simple question: what would Jesus do? He encourages his congregation to join him in making Jesus an example to be followed in specific ways in everyday life, someone who intended for us to walk as he walked, in his steps. Sheldon was a social gospel liberal who passionately, directly linked Christ to the social ills of early twentieth-century America.

In His Steps avoids making a walk like that of Jesus look easy. People who follow Jesus are often persecuted like Jesus. The theological glory of Sheldon's book is that he shows the practical consequences of making a statement such as, "Jesus is Lord."

John's Gospel has many vivid ways of showing that Christ refuses to be a bloodless abstraction. Christ's truth is personal, concrete, and incorporated, nothing less than a friend.

If you are a Methodist, you probably know that John Wesley took exemplification of Christ with great seriousness. Some contemporary Calvinists and Lutherans derided Wesley as being dangerously presumptive in teaching early Methodists that they should and could make Christ an example to be followed in their daily lives. Among Wesley's favorite books were Thomas à Kempis's *On the Imitation of Christ* and William Law's *A Serious Call to a Devout and Holy Life,* books that advocate making Jesus Lord of every moment of every day.

Wesley would surely have me add that to regard Christ as an example to be followed does not mean that Christ is a specific blueprint or a moral code. Jesus is our friend, not our detailed list of directives. You will note that in the Gospel of John, Jesus gives us surprisingly few details about how we are to act; there are no rules. Rather, following Christ as an example is a posture toward life, an inclination based upon deep, friendly affection. As Augustine said, we imitate whom we adore.

Or as Paul said, "The love of Christ urges us on" (2 Cor. 5:14). Prodded not so much through a desire to obey but rather from our desire to love the one who has loved us, "we regard no one from a human point of view" (v. 16), says Paul. As we gaze upon Christ, we are given a divine perspective. At table, as we gaze upon Christ, he transforms the way we look at Judas. Imitation of Christ emboldens Paul to claim, "If anyone is in Christ, there is a new creation: everything old has passed away; see, everything has become new!" (v. 17). In imitating whom we adore, we come more closely to resemble the object of our adoration. We are remarkably different than we would have been had we not joined Jesus at the table.

Paul says, "All this is from God, who reconciled us to himself through Christ, and has given us the ministry of reconciliation" (v. 18). Through imitation of Christ, he enlists us in his ministry of reconciliation of the world. Thus Paul can claim, "So we are ambassadors for Christ, since God is making his appeal through us" (v. 20); we are "the righteousness of God" (v. 21).

Is this enough for a full-blown life ethic? No. But it is the place where Christian ethics begins—the Son of God kneeling and washing feet. We have, in him, learned a truth about God that makes us look at things differently. As friend, Christ offers us freedom from excessive scrupulosity and worry about our behavior. We are not trying to keep our slates clean; we are acting in loving relationship, in friendship. This gives us a certain carefree freedom, with lives based not upon utility or effectiveness but upon friendship. Desiring our actions to be in accord, congruent, and complimentary with his actions, we are transformed.

Sacrament as Example

Every dinner table is the scene of service and sacrifice, if God gives us the grace to see it. We eat only because of the service of others. When, at table, I pick up a slice of bread, the staff of life, I do so as debtor. People—whose names I'll never know—tilled the soil, sowed the seed, patiently waited until the time was right, harvested the wheat, milled the flour, kneaded the dough, baked the loaf, delivered the bread, shelved it, sold it, toasted it, and presented it at table. When Alabama's legislature passed a tough immigration law that resulted in the exodus of seasonal laborers—documented and undocumented—from our state, our food prices rose considerably, and small farmers were forced out of business. Few Alabamians could be found who were willing to do the backbreaking work for the low wages. Until the fallout after the terrible law, it had not occurred to us that our low grocery prices were the result of injustice practiced against others. My life is utterly dependent upon the contributions of a host of strangers whose backbreaking labors are invisible in that slice of bread. Jesus opens our eyes to reality and tells us the truth about ourselves, God, and the world. Faith is a gift that enables us to see that our lives are sustained by gifts and grace.

So Jesus washes feet, and Peter thinks "baptism"; Jesus kneels down and washes feet, and we think of his descent into the hell of the cross. The one who serves bread and wine serves through his death. Everything we do with Jesus in the here and now means more than it appears in the here and now. And all of it is in the shape of a cross.

If this were Matthew, Mark, or Luke, words of institution along with Jesus' "do this in remembrance of me" would surely have made their way into Jesus' speech at the table. Whereas the other Gospels focus upon the memorial of Jesus in bread and wine, John focuses upon the baptismal-like deed of washing feet and Jesus' command to continue to perform such service in the future (John 13:15).

In a sense, John does his eucharistic work earlier, back in John 6, when Jesus calls himself the Bread of Life whose flesh is to be eaten and whose blood must be drunk. Think of John 13 as John's commentary on the deeper discipleship significance of Jesus' "institution" of the sacred supper of Christians. On almost every page of this Gospel, John assumes the primacy of what Christians do in bread, water, and wine and does his sacramental theology—if that's the word for it at this early stage—by what he leaves unsaid as much as by what he says.

With great subtlety here at the table John draws out the ethical significance of Christians' eating and drinking. In John, Jesus switches from the Synoptic Gospels' "do this" in bread and wine to "do this" with basin and towel. Jesus' washing of the disciples' feet is made into a symbolic commentary upon the symbol of the Eucharist, a challenge to the church every time we gather with Jesus at his table.

I love that the church doesn't ask us to get our heads straight about the deeper theological significance of Jesus and his work or doesn't insist that we get ourselves all worked up into an emotional high in order to earn the right to worship Jesus. We simply have to accept his invitation to come to his table; we only need hold out empty hands and receive his broken body, then drink his shed blood, and then invite everyone to join the feast.

Just do it, the church seems to say; God will handle the rest.

The story that John's Gospel tells is primarily a story about Jesus, the Christ, who said, "I am the light of the world" (8:12). But Matthew heard Jesus clearly say to us, "*You* are the light of the world" (Matt. 5:14, italics mine). Now, here at table, Mr. Light of the World says to us that our frail lights will shine, blinding the darkened world with their brilliance.

Jesus' commissioning of his followers is all the more remarkable because this is John's Gospel. If you read the earlier chapters of this strange work, you will note that no one—not Nicodemus, the woman at the well, the disciples, or Jesus' own mother—seems to "get it." Jesus remains to them—even after one-on-one conversation with Jesus—a great mystery. They do not understand who he is or what he says.

That Jesus would now tell these same people to imitate him, to do as he does, suggests that full comprehension and deep understanding of Jesus may not be the main point. The point is to obey Jesus, to love Jesus.

In the Rublev icon, known as *The Hospitality of Abraham* (c. 1410), three elegant divine persons cluster around a table, sharing a meal. Abraham's hospitality toward a couple of heavenly strangers is a kind of prefigurement of the three persons of the Trinity. There at table, in complete communion, are the Father, the Son, and the Holy Spirit.

And yet, if you look more closely, you see that there is an empty place on the viewer's side of the table. That empty place is reserved for you. You have a personal invitation to take your place and join in the meal with Father, Son, and Holy Spirit—even you.

Notes

1. Søren Kierkegaard, *Practice in Christianity* (Princeton: Princeton University Press, 1991), 232.

2. Ibid., 183.

3. Dietrich Bonhoeffer, *The Cost of Discipleship*, trans. R. H. Fuller (New York: Macmillan, 1949), 56.

4. Ibid., 51.

5. Charles Sheldon, *In His Steps* (Nashville: Broadman, 1935).

Lord Jesus, in your wisdom, you made our salvation social rather than solitary. By baptism you rebirthed us into a family larger and more demanding than the family into which we were born.

We confess that sometimes we wish we could save ourselves all by ourselves; salvation as a home correspondence course would be easier than having to serve you in church.

It's easier to love someone on the other side of the world than to be kind to the people seated across from us at a covered-dish supper, the ones who always bring a small dish of gray tuna noodle surprise, even though they have four children and will probably eat much more than they brought.

Why, dear Lord, must we be saved along with everyone else?

Overcome our egos. Keep showing us that just as we cannot survive by ourselves, we cannot be saved solo, that we cannot love you without loving those whom you love and for whom you gave your life. Prepare us, each time we break bread, to enter eternal life as a group.

Lord, have mercy! Amen.

CHAPTER III

MAKING LOVE IN CHURCH

"I give you a new commandment, that you love one another. Just as I have loved you, you also should love one another. By this everyone will know that you are my disciples, if you have love for one another."
—*John 13:34-35*

The *Maundy* of Maundy Thursday is an early English form of the Latin word for "mandate," referring to John 13:34. Here at the Maundy Thursday Communion table, toward the end of the supper, Jesus' last words to his followers before his betrayal, arrest, and crucifixion are our marching orders, our mandate.

A Command, Not a Suggestion

Jesus' "new commandment" may be one of the strangest aspects of this strange evening meal. *Commanded* to love? Most of us, if we ever think about this crazy thing called love, think of love primarily as a feeling, a wildly unreasonable emotion that sometimes wells up within us without premeditation.

Imagine some dear, misguided youth gazing into the eyes of his beloved, cooing to the object of his affection, "I command you to love me."

How far would he get with that?

Who would dare to command love?

Jesus, that's who. Perhaps knowing that our "love" is subject to whims and fickle emotions, Jesus commands us to "love one another." In fact, he says, "by this everyone will know that you are my disciples." Of all the commands Jesus might have made, in his last moments with his disciples— a command to believe in him as true Messiah, an edict to show courage and determination in the face of worldly opposition—the one thing he commands is "love one another."

Note that it's a *command*, not a suggestion. Having reiterated the centrality of love, Jesus now straightforwardly commands love, making love *the* defining characteristic of his followers. We are certified to have signed on with Jesus, not when we put a cross on the top of our building, not by peppering our speech with quotations from Scripture, but solely by our ability to show love to one another.

Sometimes it's easier to love a radical Muslim in Iran than a disagreeable Methodist in Iowa. In our Annual Conference, we conducted a series of "teaching moments"—our euphemism for knock-down, drag-out shouting matches—

on America's Near Eastern wars. One disputant contended, "Clergy are not experts on foreign policy" (true), and another, "The church is not supposed to be primarily about politics" (also true). Their opponent replied, "I agree with you on both of those points. The only thing we have to contribute to national political debates is the one thing they can't have through foreign policy—love."

Our most countercultural, radical gift to the way of the world is Jesus' command to love in John 13:34.

John Wesley, in his commentary on verse 34, noted that the command to love was new only "in the school of Christ."[1] Until this teaching moment at the Maundy Thursday table, Christ had not taught this "expressly." And until this moment, love had not been taught with its peculiarly Christlike twist. As Wesley said, this love was "new as to the degree," love "as I have loved you."

How much did Christ love us? After this meal we shall know—love all the way through horrible, self-sacrificing suffering unto death. How much easier for us if Jesus had simply said, "Love as much as you are able, considering all of your natural limitations"? No, to be a disciple of Jesus means to practice cruciform, self-sacrificing love, not simply because it pleases oneself, but because it pleased our Lord and Savior to command us to love. I believe that one of John Wesley's greatest contributions to the practice of the Christian faith was the explicit, organizational linkage of love of God to obedience to God.

A business executive in one of my churches told me that whenever he needs to fire someone, he takes the poor soul to a nice restaurant in order to do the deed in a public place. That way the person being given the axe can't make too much fuss.

A rather cynical abuse of a mealtime, I thought.

Jesus gathers us at the table, not only to serve us by giving us nourishment and by washing our feet but also to serve us by commanding us to "love one another," giving us an assignment so tough and demanding that it was given in public, in front of everyone so we couldn't squirm out of it, and at a meal in order to soften the blow of it.

Help with the Loving

Lest you despair at his sweeping command to love, remember that it is within this setting that Jesus promises to send the Holy Spirit who gives us what we need to be obedient to Jesus' command. He doesn't expect us to love on our own.

We are now at the core of the mission of Jesus and also of the church. In my church, amid widespread membership and attendance decline, we have recently stressed the necessity of the church being obedient to the "Great Commission"—in Matthew 28, in which Jesus commissions us to go into all the world and make disciples through baptism and teaching. Some say that the church puts more stress on the evangelistic Great Commission than on the prophetic

Great Commandment to "love one another" here in John 13:34.

Here in the Great Commandment to love one another Jesus implicitly links our behavior in the church with the church's commission to go out into the world to make disciples. As youth we sang "They'll Know We Are Christians by Our Love." The song, as I recall, was a bit sappy, if not downright self-satisfied in its declarations that "we will love one another." But still, tell me if you think Jesus says otherwise in John 13.

In my efforts at evangelism, the greatest impediment to reaching the world and making disciples for Christ is the church. Many times I've presented my argument for following Jesus Christ, only to have the recipient counter, "After I experienced a horrible fight in the church in which I grew up, I haven't been back."

One of my pastors has a ministry in which he does a Bible study and discussion twice a week at a local bar. He had a dozen professions of faith and baptisms arise from the conversations he has held in that bar. When I commented that a pastor doing Bible study in a bar was unconventional, he countered, "Tell it to Jesus. As I recall, he did some of his best teaching at a table accompanied by a jug of wine."

OK, so evangelism through bread and wine has occurred before. But when I asked him the focus of most of his conversations in the bar, he replied, "Well, maybe it's because it's Alabama, but when people find out I'm a preacher, then invariably we've got to spend an hour or so with everyone telling their horror stories about how they got abused and wounded in some little rural church.

"I tire of these stories of congregations behaving badly, but it's like I've got to hear all this before I have the chance to say, 'I'm sorry that happened to you in a church. We're sinners who are being saved by Jesus and sometimes our sin gets the best of us. Are you willing to give Jesus' people another try?'"

Sometimes people can't see the love of Christ because of the unloving behavior of those whom Christ has clearly commanded to love one another.

Our efforts to obey Christ's Great Commission would have greater effect if we were faithful to the whole of what Christ said to us in Matthew 28. There Jesus says not only that we are to go into all the world and make disciples, not only that we are to baptize everyone, but also that we are to teach them "all that I have commanded," including the command to love.

Churches often put signs in front of their buildings, giving the times of services, and they often include a little slogan such as, "The Church with a Warm Heart in the Heart of the City." Imagine a church sign that proclaimed, "Come Join Us. We'll Teach You *Everything* Christ Commanded." We will hold nothing back from you, including the commands to turn the other cheek, to forgive seventy-times-seven times, and to give to everyone who asks. We'll teach you everything Christ commanded including the commandment to love other disciples as much as he has loved us.

Saint Jerome said that the once-eloquent Saint John in his dotage was reduced to simply repeating over and over again, "My little children, love one another."[2]

This is how others know "you are my disciples," says Jesus (John 13:35). One of the first apologists for the Christian faith, Tertullian, says that this was the major reason why the church defeated the Roman Empire without firing a shot or raising a single platoon. The world looked at the church and exclaimed, "See how these Christians love one another."[3] Alas, too many now say, "See how these Christians fight like cats and dogs with one another."

Jesus commanded love on his way to suffering incredibly because of his love for us. The world loves until there is suffering; Jesus walked the way of suffering love. Martin Luther King Jr. considered love a real possibility, a potent political weapon, but not without suffering. In a 1967 Christmas Eve sermon, King virtually boasted that his followers, in the spirit of Jesus, could out-suffer, out-love, and out-endure any capacity of his racist opponents to hurt or to hate.

Loving Those Who Love God

When Jesus says, in John 13:34, "I give you a new commandment, that you love one another," the love is applied only within the community of believers, never to love of the neighbor in general or love of the enemy. Love, in John's

Gospel, implies no duties toward the world, only the duty to keep safe from the world's corruption and to tell the world that it is wrong about Jesus; Jesus is Light, a Word from God to the benighted world about the world's salvation, the "message we have heard from him and proclaim to you" (1 John 1:1-5). Some have taken this tendency of the Gospel of John to be delimiting and isolationist, a parochial confinement of Jesus' outrageous enemy-forgiving love that characterizes the other Gospels.

One would be hard pressed to construct a distinct picture of the Christian life if one were limited only to the Fourth Gospel with no Sermon on the Mount and to limited practical guidance on how disciples are to comport ourselves in the real world.

Remember that John's greater concern is to contend with the world's popular definitions of the "real world." We cannot limit ourselves, when reading John's account of the Maundy Thursday (or anything else in John), to explicitly didactic content. A fuller reading of the story is necessary if you want to derive specific ethical, practical inferences from the Fourth Gospel. If you are a person who desires immediately to know the practical implications of things, always asking, in response to some religious declaration, "Well, so what?" then you may be frustrated by John's presentation of Jesus.

John does ethics, not with lists of ethical injunctions, the way Paul often does ethics, but rather through stories. Any ethic derived from the Fourth Gospel will be by implication, by watching Jesus at work in the world, by hearing stories about him, and then by attempting to stumble after him.

For instance, we have noted that Jesus, in one of his rare moments of explicit ethical demand in this Gospel, says that we ought to wash the feet of others just as he has done. But we make a mistake if we take that as a specific directive for the whole of Christian life. John Wesley, in his commentary on John 13, asked, "Why do we not read of any one apostle ever washing the feet of any other?" Then he answered, because "they understood their Lord better. They knew he never designed that this should be taken literally." Wesley knew that, typical of the Fourth Gospel, foot washing stood for something larger than mere foot washing. Through these stories, John gives believers a posture toward the world, a perspective, the secret to God's identity, and the inside line on what's really going on in the world.

Many have been bothered that John's repeated stress on love as the whole point of Christian life doesn't seem to be primarily love of the neighbor in need in the world but love of one another in the church.

I think it important to note that John believes that loving one another in the church is a means of not only enacting his love for his followers but also of witnessing to the whole world. Jesus dies for the sake of the whole world (John 1:29; 3:16). "God so loved the church that…"? No. "God so loved the world that God gave…" (3:16).

For this is the message you have heard from the beginning, that we should love one another. . . . We know love by this, that he laid down his life for us—and we ought to lay down our lives for one another. How does God's love abide in anyone who has the world's goods and sees a brother or sister in need and yet refuses help? Little children, let us love, not in word or speech, but in truth and action.
—1 John 3:11, 16-18

John has Jesus focus intensely on how we are to behave with fellow disciples. If we love Jesus, we're commanded to love fellow followers of Jesus. If we can't somehow find a way to love Jesus' friends, we'll never figure out how to love Jesus.

In my experience, John gets it right. Interrelationships among Christians may be the toughest love assignment Jesus gives us. I know that I've found it easier to have positive feelings for Muslims than for some of my fellow Methodists. Sometimes it's easier to love neighbors across the ocean than the annoying guy next door.

Jesus here speaks tenderly to his disciples as "little children." The phrase occurs in the Gospel of John only here but is a frequent phrase in 1 John (in 2:1; 2:12; and seven times more in the few chapters of 1 John). I wonder if calling us "little children" is more than merely a tender term of endearment; it's an all-too-accurate description of us church people who, though we are called to be children of God, often fight among ourselves like a bunch of unruly, spoiled brats.

I suppose that's when we give thanks that our Lord said, "Let the little children [the spoiled, bickering-among-themselves, immature brats] come to me" (Luke 18:16).

Those who say, "I love God," and hate their brothers or sisters, are liars; for those who do not love a brother or sister whom they have seen, cannot love God whom they have not seen. The commandment we have from him is this; those who love God must love their brothers and sisters also.

—*1 John 4:20-21*

It is tough to love fellow Christians, especially when engaged in fierce disagreements with fellow Christians about doctrine or social issues. I was present during a fierce debate over the issue of sexual orientation and its significance for the ordination of church leaders. During the debate, one of the disputants said, "I'm sorry, but this is a matter of upholding Scripture and I love the Bible."

His antagonist countered, "Well, you are not commanded to love the Bible; you are commanded to love your Christian brothers and sisters!" Surely he was thinking of the Gospel and the letters of John.

To be fair, John doesn't have Jesus say that loving one another in the church means that there won't be acrid disagreements with one another. Tertullian says that the world marveled at Christians' ability to love one another, but Tertullian was a crabby and combative antagonist with his fellow Christians; loving one another means more than merely agreeing with one another. I have served churches in which, rather than love one another, we decided to have a truce with one another. That meant that it was very difficult to have disagreements with one another because we were fearful that the church would disintegrate during our arguments.

I've seen marriages that were so weak that the couple couldn't have a good argument. Churches can be like that too. So let us note that Jesus doesn't command us just to get along with one another or tolerate one another—Christ's people must love one another as deeply as Christ loves us.

As a bishop, I occasionally had to receive the credentials of clergy calling it quits. Never once did I have a Methodist preacher throw in the towel because of Jesus. One would think that there would be many preachers who say, "I give up! I can't continue to work for the Word Made Flesh. Jesus is just too demanding!"

More typical is for clergy on their way out to say, "I love Jesus but can't stand his friends." They're committed to church in general, but specifically they desire to choke to death the chair of the Altar Guild.

I left academia to become a bishop. Sometimes people asked, "What do you most miss about life in the university, compared with your life now as church bureaucrat?"

I answered: "I miss most the Duke Office of Admissions. The university admissions office insured that I would never be forced to work with anyone who was not like me—with the same background and the same gifts for manipulating the system to my advantage. Church, however, is notoriously nonselective. We pastors are forced to work with anybody whom Jesus drags in the door!"

"Spirituality" is all the rage—feeling religious, sort of, without the bother of having to be religious with people who are not as vaguely spiritual as you. Spirituality is Jesus without the messiness of having to live with the people Jesus loves!

I led a clergy conference in Hawaii. Before the meeting, we toured the islands as sightseers. The guide told us, "Hawaii is a tropical paradise. Here, unlike where you're from, all these ethnic groups live in love and harmony."

I believed it. Then I met with the pastors. Harmony? They complained of disjointed congregations in which the Japanese think they're better than the Koreans, the Koreans look down on the Samoans, and everyone detests the Japanese as much as they despise the Anglos, along with high rates of drug abuse and shocking poverty.

Leave it to the clergy, I thought—enmeshed in the church—to discover the ugly underbelly of paradise.

I asked one of my M.Div. students, "Why are you headed toward ministry?"

He answered, "Because I enjoy working with people."

I replied, "Dear, have you actually met any of the people with whom you will be working? What sort of masochist finds enjoyment in that?"

In making clear that Jesus' act of service must be replicated in the lives of his disciples, we have an unusually ethically explicit moment in the rather vague and symbolic Gospel of John. That explicitness is surely a sign of how important the command to love is in the Fourth Gospel. When I consider Jesus' frequent, boring repetition of the words *love one another*—clearly meaning love the person seated next to you at the Lord's Table—I think that maybe Jesus sometime served a United Methodist church. You know us preachers: we tend to commend those virtues that the church lacks. The way that both John and Paul construe Jesus' *love your neighbor* to apply to relations among believers suggests that both John and Paul served time trying to act like Jesus in United Methodist congregations (Rom. 13:8-10; Gal. 5:14).

Divine Love

And yet it is also clear that John means these mysterious, ethically charged actions to be read as much more than simple humanitarian beneficence. Being washed by Jesus is more than a model of service (John 13:14-15) for the disciples. It is also to be taken up into the mysterious movement of his cross (vv. 7, 8b, 10). The one who commands us to go and do likewise is none other than the Word Made Flesh. Jesus builds his repeated Johannine ethical commands to love one another upon his primal sacramental command to love him. The great grace that enables a Christian to love, of all people, fellow Christians, flows from love of and love for Christ. To love as he loves is to be washed by Jesus. As Jesus is being diabolically betrayed by one of his twelve best friends at the table, he again promises always to be faithful to his friends, enabling us to love him and our neighbors because he has first loved us (1 John 4:19).

In John's Gospel, Jesus is the man from heaven. He is not someone who is born in Bethlehem; he is an extraterrestrial, a veritable ET, who gathers a little group of disciples around him and says strange things to them. Born "from above" (John 3:3), he is on his way to someplace else to prepare a place for them. His humanity is genuine (1:4), but he is "from above." He is the friend who is always the "other." If your artistic bent enabled you to like both the otherworldly mysteriousness of the movie *Avatar* and gritty realism of *J. Edgar*, you are a great candidate for John's Jesus.

John's Gospel therefore keeps everything tied to theology. Any claims that John makes for us as followers of Jesus are tied to John's claims about what God is doing in Jesus. Unlike in the other Gospels, the main moral concern in John's Gospel is not in the law and its proper messianic interpretation. John cares about "life in his name" (20:31, and so on). Life in the name of Jesus—a revelation of God's love for the world—is a life of love. As the "Father loves the Son" (5:20 and so on), so the Son "loved his own" (13:1, 13:34, and so on), and so we are to "love one another as I have loved you" (15:12).

Love here arises out of Christology. Jesus—in his actions and in his words—defines love rather than our vague, mushy, adulterated "love" defining Jesus. Jesus' "new commandment" (13:34) to love at first sounds nice until we see Jesus' love in action forgiving his enemies while hanging on the cross and washing his enemies' feet at the table.

Love with Basin and Towel Defining the Spiritual

Frankly, we prefer *love* without clear definition. When John has words like *love* and *spirit* take bodily form in the words and deeds of Jesus, we get nervous.

Spiritual tends to be synonymous with *vague*. For instance, in a January 2011 interview with Piers Morgan, Oprah Winfrey announced that her most important role is "spiritual leader": "This isn't about me. I am the messenger to deliver the message of redemption, of hope, of forgiveness, of gratitude, of evolving people to the best of themselves. So I am on my personal journey...to fulfill the highest expression of myself here as a human being here on earth," said Oprah. Oprah is now not only the savviest of business persons but also the national leader of the burgeoning "I'm (vaguely) religious but not (bodily) spiritual" movement.

I hear John ask, "What, in Jesus' name, hath this 'spiritual' to do with the Christian faith?"

In his sermon on the Sermon on the Mount, Martin Luther notes that Jesus begins his sermon on the First Beatitude by attacking "the greatest and most universal belief or religion on earth"—those "crazy saints" who think that the purpose of the Christian faith is spiritual aggrandizement (Matt. 5:3).[4] Luther says that Jesus makes "blessed are the poor in spirit" the First Beatitude because, if at the beginning of the sermon one feels that one is spiritually well endowed, spiritually rich, then by the end of the sermon—after the preacher has pummeled you for marrying after divorce, looking at a person lustfully, not turning the other cheek, and returning evil for evil—everybody looks spiritually destitute!

So the first thing to say to those dear, sweet folk who (when invited to sign on to the Lord's Table as a means of grace) say, "I'm not religious, but I'm very spiritual," is,

"Where the heck did you get the idea that Christianity gave a rip about either religion or spirituality?"

Spirituality is another means of turning faith in God into a commodity for our private consolation. This privatization of God was done by the modern democratic, liberal nation-state in order to neutralize Christianity, to marginalize it from the common life, to bury God in the confines of the self, to trivialize the Trinity, and to keep this governmentally troubling faith from going public. It's hard not to suspect that what passes today for spirituality was invented in order to silence the church in order to make way for the omnipotent state and its capitalist economy. The government has found that Christians (well, any believer who thinks that his or her God might be more important than the state) are easier to manage if they will confine their faith to something within.

So having never heard John do "spiritual," vast numbers of Americans run around thinking that religion is vague and personal. In an attempt to rescue some shred of the Christian faith from the ravages of the modern world, the German theologian Friedrich Schleiermacher thinned the gospel down: the essence of religion is not thought or action but feeling and intuition, faith that dare not utter its name, and religion that is felt but seldom seen. God is forced to retreat from the stage of history and to work exclusively within the confines of the modern self.[5]

Thanks to folk like Schleiermacher, spirituality has made

religion successful and safe, enabling 90 percent of all Americans to say that they believe in God. If you crank *God* down low enough, make the term vague enough, and empty it of any intellectual content, everybody is a believer. Spirituality enables us to be the first generation of Christians in history who cannot get hurt by following Jesus.

I think John would back me up in saying that spirituality is but our most recent attempt to mitigate demands of having God come to us as Christ. Revelation is reduced to a class of phenomena that some individuals experience more dramatically than others, an innate something or other within. We have thus found a way to give credence to Ludwig Feuerbach's claim that *God* is another name for the projection of the deepest human desires. Thus Karl Barth warned, "Whoever is concerned with the spirit, the heart, and conscience, and...inwardness...must be confronted with the question of whether he is really concerned with God and not with the apotheosis of man."[6]

Barth believed that we know humanity only on the basis of what we know of God in Jesus Christ. Spirituality gets it the other way around, beginning with human subjectivity and asking what we can know of God based upon what we know of ourselves. Christians may not know everything, but we do know Jesus Christ is God's self-definition. Spirituality, in its present form (a pale, cobbled-together imitation of that risky piety once practiced by the saints), is but our latest effort to fashion a God more congenial to how our God ought to look if God were worthy of worship by people like us.

My theory is that when *Christian spirituality* no longer meant "piety," it ran unchecked and untethered to any ethical substance. Today, *God* means whatever we want *God* to mean, whatever is practically helpful to us in our pursuit of whatever it was we want more than God, whatever, whomever we find credible within the limits of modern imagination. Christians historically thought of their piety, not primarily as a technique to get them up to God but rather as God's appointed means to get down to them. Much that passes for spirituality in our age begins with the claim to complete ignorance of who God actually is. Not knowing God in the flesh (John 1), our age knows nothing of God. "God? Oh, I can't say anything for sure about God. That would be intellectually arrogant."[7]

We wish. Christology gives specific, unavoidable, prophetic content and necessary theological control to pneumatology. Our imaginations are prone to fanciful constructions of God. Incarnational faith in the Word Made Flesh regards "faith" as less interesting than "faith *in whom?*" Solid, interesting, intellectual content is precisely what is lacking in so many contemporary treatments of spirituality.

For Christians, "God is God, not in the mists of some transcendence, not on the basis of their own opinion, thought, or speculation, not in the form of an image projected by them, but in Jesus Christ," thunders Karl Barth.[8]

I know this is a prejudiced ecclesiastical statement (the only kind you should expect a preacher to make), but whenever I hear the now commonplace, "I'm spiritual but not religious," my reaction is similar to the one I had to generations of Duke students who pled, "Since we love each other, why do we need to stand up in a church and say it? Can't we just live together without all that marriage stuff?"

Because *I love you* so often means in this culture, "I love me and want to use you to love me even more," the church has found it helpful to test our declarations of love by submitting them to the specific vows of marriage. Can your love endure the test of a lifelong, exclusive, morally formative promise? The main difference between love as a romantic infatuation and love as an enduring commitment is a promise to love.

Note that, in the Service of Marriage, the pastor doesn't ask, "John, do you feel like you love Susan?" The question is, "John *will you* love Susan?" *Love* is here defined as an act of the will, something we decide to do, a gift that we promise to give.

"So you say that you are 'spiritual'? Any specific flesh or muscle on that 'spirit' whom you worship? Can your 'faith' in God endure the test of obedience to a first-century Jew who lived briefly, worked on us at his last time at table with us, died violently, and returned unexpectedly? Are you able to love God without despising those whom God loves?" If not, why bother?

Notes

1. John Wesley, *Notes on the New Testament,* http://wesley.nnu.edu /john-wesley/john-wesleys-notes-on-the-bible/notes-on-the-gospel-accord ing-to-st-john/#Chapter+XIII.

2. Jerome, *Ad Galatianos* 3.6.10.

3. Tertullian, *Apology* 39.7.

4. Martin Luther, "The Sermon on the Mount and the Magnificat," vol. 21 of *Luther's Works*, American Edition, ed. Jaroslav Pelikan and Helmut T. Lehmann (St. Louis: Concordia, 1955–86), 11–19.

5. Barth said that Schleiermacher made Spirit "identical with subjective stimulation," a merely "supreme enhancement" of the human spirit that eventually degenerated, in Barth's estimation, to Ernst Troeltsch's equation of the Holy Spirit with "direct religious productivity of the individual." Cited in Eberhard Busch, *The Great Passion: An Introduction to Karl Barth's Theology*, trans. Geoffrey W. Bromiley, ed. Darrell L. Guder and Judith J. Guder (Grand Rapids, Mich.: Eerdmans, 2004), 221.

6. Karl Barth, in his introductory essay to Ludwig Feuerbach, *The Essence of Christianity* (New York: Harper and Brothers, 1957), xxiv.

7. Kant, precursor to Schleiermacher, said, "I had to do away with knowledge in order to make room for faith." Kant, *Critique of Pure Reason*, trans. Norman Kemp Smith (New York: St. Martin's Press, 1965), 29.

8. Karl Barth, *The Christian Life: Church Dogmatics IV/4, Lecture Fragments*, trans. Geoffrey W. Bromiley (Grand Rapids, Mich.: Eerdmans, 1981), 93.

Lord Jesus, all we want is cheap groceries. We don't intend for others to suffer to provide our bread.

All we want is a quick bite to eat with our close friends. We don't expect to be bitten by your truth told at the table.

All we desire is quiet time with you to share what's on our hearts, to enumerate for you our multiple aches and pains. We don't expect to be told the truth by you, certainly don't plan to receive an assignment from you.

All we want is to be saved by you, so we're surprised to be commandeered by you, even when we are at the table with you.

Lord, defeat our expectations. Christ, have mercy upon us. Amen.

CHAPTER IV

TRUTH AT THE TABLE

After saying this Jesus was troubled in spirit, and declared, "Very truly, I tell you, one of you will betray me." The disciples looked at one another, uncertain of whom he was speaking. One of his disciples—the one whom Jesus loved—was reclining next to him; Simon Peter therefore motioned to him to ask Jesus of whom he was speaking. So while reclining next to Jesus, he asked him, "Lord, who is it?" Jesus answered, "It is the one to whom I give this piece of bread when I have dipped it in the dish." So when he had dipped the piece of bread, he gave it to Judas son of Simon Iscariot. After he received the piece of bread, Satan entered into him. Jesus said to him, "Do quickly what you are going to do."... So, after receiving the piece of bread, he immediately went out. And it was night.
—John 13:21-30

And it was night" (13:30)—with these evocative words, John ends his account of the Maundy Thursday meal. Jesus, "troubled in spirit," has predicted betrayal by his own disciples, Satan has run amuck among Jesus' closest friends, and now they depart into the night. Early Christians called their central act of worship the Lord's Supper, not only in remembrance of this nocturnal meal in which "the Lord Jesus on the night when he was betrayed took a loaf of bread" (1 Cor. 11:23), but also because the church first worshiped on the evening of the first day of the Jewish workweek, Sunday, the day of Jesus' resurrection, when people got off work.

Shepherds working the night shift were the first to be told the news of Jesus' birth. Jesus did some of his most significant work at night, stilling storms at sea and striding out upon the waves to save his disciples (Mark 4:37). John says that Nicodemus came to Jesus "by night" (John 3:2). On Maundy Thursday evening, Jesus tells his disciples to "do quickly what you are going to do" (13:27), perhaps knowing that the cowardly work in which they will engage is best done under the cover of darkness.

Though early Christians worshiped in the evening, my church doesn't do well at night. I have memories growing up in a church that had Sunday evening and Wednesday evening worship, but that seems a long time ago. My church now prefers to worship in the warm, bright light of the midday sun with upbeat music and bubbly, cheerful singers, all led by us cheerful, grinning clergy.

Though the actual resurrection of Jesus occurred while it was still dark, sometime before the women came out to his tomb in the darkness, somehow we tend to think that God refuses to work the night shift. Religion is the fun that we have on happy, sunny days, not the terrors that sometimes afflict us in the dead of night. When I asked a woman why she had not been attending church lately, she replied, "I'm going through a rather dark time in my life just now, and the last place I want to be is at my confoundedly happy church."

John says simply, "It was night," and somehow we know that he means more than the setting of the sun.

Of course, John opens his Gospel by saying that Jesus is the "light [shining] in the darkness" (1:5), but there is something about the light of Christ that cannot be fully comprehended without our also being honest about the darkness, our bleak failure to comprehend the light shining out toward us in our stumbling in the dark. Night is the time of vulnerability. Jesus doesn't stay in the warm glow of fellowship about the table. He goes forth into the darkness, daring the night. And we can't be with him unless we go with him.

One of You Will Betray

No sooner had we settled in at the table that night than Jesus dropped his bombshell: "One of you will betray me." Leonardo da Vinci painted that awful moment in his *Last Supper*, that shocking, horrible time of truth. In Leonardo's masterpiece, as Jesus—serene and dolorous, "troubled in spirit" (same word for when Jesus was "troubled" by the death of his friend Lazarus, John 11:33)—pronounces the words, all the disciples draw back in revulsion, push away from the table of accusation, and jump to their feet in shock.

63

And all have the effrontery to ask indignantly, "Lord, who would do such a horrible deed?"

Note that John says they "looked at one another, uncertain of whom he was speaking" (13:22). Isn't that typical of us? When judgment comes our way, we instinctively attempt to deflect the accusation to the person seated next to us.

When a student at the church's nearby college joined with a couple of other students and burned a dozen rural churches to the ground—apparently just for the hell of it—a student leader told me that he was surprised by phone calls from reporters from all over the country. The purpose of these calls was to ask, "Did you ever hear the guy say hateful things about religion?" No. "Did he seem unusually angry?" No. "Do you think he was crazed by drug abuse?" No.

"Actually, he was just a regular guy," the student said. "He looked and acted just like us." Oh, how much easier evil would be if it were limited to people totally unlike us!

During the first days of the Penn State University child molestation scandal, a friend and I were discussing the events.

"The behavior of the students that first night in state college, the rioting and hooliganism was terrible," I said.

"That's just what I would have expected someone your age to say," my friend replied. "This scandal wasn't produced by any of the students; the sins were all committed by guys our age."

I love that Leonardo painted his *Last Supper* on the wall of Santa Maria delle Grazia, where the monks took their meals and were forced occasionally to look up from their tables (reserved for "the religious") and to connect their monastic table with that of Jesus and his betrayers. Ouch.

Table of Truth

Of the many meals that Jesus ate with his disciples, his last supper occupies a central place in the imagination of the church. Last meals are revealing.

Texas prison officials have decided to terminate the tradition of special last meals for inmates facing execution. They have responded to the public outcry after Lawrence Brewer, forty-four years old, requested a large dinner before his lethal injection. Brewer, a white supremacist, had been convicted of killing James Byrd Jr., a forty-nine-year-old black man, by dragging him behind his pickup truck until he died.

Mr. Brewer's final meal request was as follows:

> a pound of barbecue with half a loaf of white bread; three fajitas "with fixings"; a cheese omelet with "ground beef, tomatoes, onions, bell peppers and jalapenos"; two chicken fried steaks "smothered in gravy with sliced onions"; a "triple meat" bacon cheeseburger with "fixings on the side"; a "large bowl" of fried okra; a "meat lovers" pizza; a pint of vanilla ice cream; a "slab" of peanut butter fudge with crushed peanuts; and three root beers.[1]

Though he was given some of the items, he ate nothing.

Brian D. Price, a former inmate who as jailhouse chef cooked last meals for 218 prisoners on death row in Texas, offered to prepare meals for the condemned for free. Officials told him that he had cooked his last, last meal. Chef Price urged the legislature to restore the last meals, saying, "No, these people don't deserve a last meal request, but we as a society have to show that softer side, that compassion. It's bad enough that we have the death penalty, it's so archaic, but then to turn around and say, 'No, we're not going to feed you,' just out of pure meanness.... We have to show that we are not distorting that justice with revenge.'"[2]

In other words, Price contends that we ought to provide a last meal for the condemned, not primarily from compassion for the humanity of those whom we execute, but rather to show some vestige of humanity in us, the executioners.

Jesus, on his way to his death, spends his last supper with friends who shall betray him. He serves them as host, washing their feet. He, who could have reacted to their betrayal with revenge, acts with compassion. But he also redefines our notions of compassion by telling them the truth.

We cannot sup with Jesus if we won't risk being told the truth by Jesus. At the heart of Christian worship is the warm, loving experience of coming close to Jesus, becoming cozy with Christ, snuggling up to him in worshipful affection and adoration. But Jesus has a way of making worship "in spirit" also a matter of worship "in truth" (John 4:24). We gather to have a jubilant "praise service" only to have the One who is not only the way and the life but also the truth serve us by smacking us in the face with the truth we've spent all week avoiding.

As a student in South Carolina in the 1960s, not too sure about the church, wondering if Christian ministry might be a waste of time, I was in a little Methodist church on a Sunday when the Lord's Supper was to be celebrated. We plodded through a rather predictable service until, just before we were invited to the Lord's Table, the preacher paused and said, "Sadly, those of us who gather at the altar to eat with Jesus refuse to eat at a dime-store lunch counter with brothers and sisters whose skin isn't the same color as ours. God forgive us."

Ouch.

Maybe his truth—even when it's the truth of our betrayals—is so severe that it ought not be uttered except at his table, truth that can't be faced except in the context of his love and his gift. Jesus has been expounding, through many long chapters in John's Gospel, his love for us, barely mentioning any of our myriad of sins against him. With tireless reiteration he has spoken of his affection for his disciples. So what he says about his disciples' betrayal is said only in the context of his prior statements about his love for us even unto death.

Thus the theologian Karl Barth says that grace always precedes judgment: first the strong declaration of God's love, doing for us what we cannot do for ourselves, then mention of our sin. The truth of God cannot be received by someone who is insecure, who is uncertain of just where she stands with God. Only the securely loved have the ability to hear, really hear, of their failures to love.

I noted this early in my own ministry. Our church re-instituted monthly Communion (they had celebrated the Lord's Supper a grand total of once—Maundy Thursday—before I got there). In my yearly evaluation of my preaching, I noted to my surprise that I preached some of my most truthful, tough, "prophetic" sermons on those Communion Sundays. Somehow the Lord's Supper gave me permission not to overly qualify everything I said and just let the truth rip, as truth had been given to me.

Looking back, I think that I unconsciously knew that Communion is the ideal locale for "prophetic" preaching. That the one who preaches the tough truth from the pulpit is also the one who confesses to equality in hunger and then offers the gifts of God for the people of God at the altar, sets divine judgment in the context of divine grace.

Table of Judgment

Though Jesus brings us into the presence of some tough, demanding, judging truth, let's also remember his words: "I came not to judge the world, but to save the world" (John 12:47). "He [Christ] shall come to judge the living and the dead," we say in the Apostles' Creed. There shall be a future time when Christ will pass judgment on all people. John has the distinctive conviction that the judgment has already occurred in Jesus' encounter with the world.

"Indeed, God did not send the Son into the world to condemn the world, but in order that the world might be saved through him. Those who believe in him are not condemned; but those who do not believe are condemned already, because they have not believed in the name of the only Son of God. And this is the judgment, that the light has come into the world, and people loved darkness rather than light because their deeds were evil."
—*John 3:17-19*

Being at the table with Jesus tends to be an experience of judgment. We need not wait until some future assize; whenever and wherever Jesus is present, we are brought face-to-face with our sin and also with Christ's forgiveness of our sin and his willingness to eat and drink with sinners. And the judgment he made upon us was to love us.

John also asserts that the Holy Spirit is Jesus' continuing presence with us in the community of faith. One reason why Jesus did not get more worked up over the death of his friend Lazarus (11:38-44) is that his friend's death was no match for Jesus' love. Eternal life is now: "I am the resurrection and the life. Those who believe in me, even though they die, will live, and everyone who lives and believes in me will never die" (11:25-26). We need not cool our heels throughout this life in expectation of some better, future life in which we will eventually be closer to Christ than we are in the present loneliness. Life with Christ is now: "We know that we have passed from death to life because we love one another" (1 John 3:14). Whenever in the church we manage—in spite of all obstacles—to love one another, we experience eternal life.

As Emily Dickinson wrote in a poem, when we think about the presence of Christ, we "blunder" if we think that "Eternity is *Then*." No, after the Resurrection, "No friend have I that so persists, / As this Eternity."[3] In Christ, eternity is present as a quality and mode of life here. Believers are free from dread of some future time of judgment, having already seen the true face of God's judgment as the face of the loving Christ. We also do not spend our days here longing for God's future rescue of us from this "veil of tears" and our placement in some "better place" where we will at last be with God. United with Christ, because of his presence with us here, now, we live with freedom and confidence.

True, we tend to experience that eternal life in fits and starts, episodically in the church whenever we are given the grace to love one another. We believe that these glimpses of eternity shall one day be ours forever.

Knowing, Not Knowing Jesus

On another evening, Jesus welcomed a distinguished visitor for nocturnal conversation: Nicodemus (John 3:1-21).

John says many people were attracted to Jesus who were dazzled by his miraculous signs, but Jesus revealed himself to none of them because their faith was shallow (2:25), implying that the lust for miraculous verification of faith is small minded and thin. Right after dissing shallow-thinking people, John introduces us to thoughtful Nicodemus. Nicodemus doesn't have a good Jewish name such as Nathaniel (gift/God). Nicodemus has a classical Greek name (victory/people). He is a Pharisee, a scholar of Torah. So this evening, Jesus converses with a cultured, classically educated scholar. (Nicodemus comes to Jesus "by night," and this suggests to me that he may be not only a cultured, Jewish, Greek-influenced Hellenistic scholar but also possibly a young person because young adults' brains are not fully in gear until after sunset).

Nicodemus is identified as a "leader of the Jews"—the powerful religious authorities who have engaged Jesus in bitter debate throughout the Gospel of John.

The first thing that Nicodemus says to Jesus is braggadocio about his intellectual achievements: "We know that…"; "Research shows that…"; "A recent, important monograph successfully proves that…" Nicodemus, after thoughtful consideration, has pegged Jesus as "a teacher come from God." A teacher. That's a high compliment for someone with Nicodemus's credentials who is probably more accustomed to teaching than to being taught. Nicodemus is much like some of my educated, though godless, academic buddies who say, "I will grant that Jesus is a great moral example, a wonderful teacher, but don't you think you Christians are going a bit overboard in calling him *God*?"

The late pop atheist Christopher Hitchens said that although he thinks Christians are goofy for thinking Jesus is divine, he was willing to grant that Jesus is a much-better-than-average teacher. Hitchens died while I was writing this book. Presumably Hitchens now knows firsthand that Jesus is considerably more than he was earlier unable to believe.

Jesus doesn't even acknowledge Nicodemus's flattering opening shot: "We know that you are a great teacher." Rather he shoots back a wild non sequitur: "You've got to be born from above!"

After an awkward gap—"Ok, how can this be?"—there follows again a non sequitur from Jesus: "You must be born from above by water and the spirit."

Nicodemus: "How?"

Jesus: "The spirit, or wind—take it as you like—blows where it will."

"What?"

Note, dear reader, how quickly Jesus has moved this sophisticated, Hellenistic scholar from the self-assured "We know" to the befuddled "How can this be?" Jesus, who was introduced to us in the beginning of this Gospel as Mr. Light of the World, has quickly put this enlightened inquirer in the dark.

Nicodemus wonders: When Jesus says *water*, is Jesus referring to amniotic fluid of the womb or to the water of baptism? When Jesus says *wind*, is he using the Greek *pneuma* in the ordinary sense of *wind* or in the more theological sense of *spirit*?

Who knows? Jesus explains nothing.

As a religious authority (like Nicodemus, a full-time student of scripture), I can tell you: Jesus takes delight in the discombobulation of people who lead most conversations with, "We know…"

Nicodemus begins, not with a question, but rather with a declaration, an intellectual assertion: *we know.* That's the whole purpose of bothering with education: to know. Is this not the reason not only for the modern university but also for the whole modern world? René Descartes urged us, through systematic doubt, to free ourselves from the intellectual baggage of the past, to reject received knowledge, to search for certitude, and in Immanuel Kant's words, to "Dare to know!" The goal of the empirical method is, through the application of systemic doubt, to reach certitude? *We know.* The world seeks sure, solid, foundational knowledge on which to stand.

What is the purpose of astronomical university tuition? What is the purpose of higher education and talented young adults scurrying to class, tutored by aged, wise faculty? To produce people who face the perplexities of the world with a BS degree and the confident, "We know."

I have a friend who did her master's thesis on the mission statements of U.S. colleges in the past 100 years. In the nineteenth century, most colleges said that they existed to impart "wisdom" to their students. By the early twentieth century, the promise of "wisdom" had been reduced in mission statements to a more modest offer of "knowledge." Then colleges began promising students "information." She predicts that in a few years, colleges will advertise with, "Come study with us and we will give you lots of data."

"What you don't know about AIDS can kill you," said the poster. Knowledge equals power, which means control.

73

Why are evil and heartache in the world? Ignorance! People who don't know. That's what well-educated, white Southerners said, in my part of the world, back in the 1960s when there were bombings in Birmingham: "We know that we are not responsible for this racist violence. We know it's not us; it's these ignorant rednecks. We know that education is the answer."

Now I suspect that some of you reading this book would love for me to demonstrate to your satisfaction that Jesus is a "great teacher," a philosopher who enunciated some noble principles for the purpose-driven life, a spiritual guru with some original insights that you can use in your daily work rather than to assert with John that Jesus is Mr. Light of the World, Son of God, Eternal Word who wants to use you rather than to be used by you. You would like for me to make Jesus a teacher because, well, that would make Jesus more manageable, leaving us in the driver's seat.

And I would like nothing better than to reassure you that Jesus Christ could be helpful in this culturally approved, governmentally subsidized project otherwise known as education. We know!

Well, unfortunately for this project it's the Gospel of John, and we are thinking about Jesus. Jesus is the Son of God who specializes in taking knowledgeable "we know" sort of people and in just a couple of sentences reducing them to "But, but, how can this be?" people.

And though Jesus can be abrasive to people who really want to be "in the know," for those of you who might desire a wider sort of epistemology than the thin, constricted stuff that passes for thinking these days, Jesus can be a real pain.

No wonder that early interpreters of John knew that he was displaying the "more" that was behind or within historical events from the earthly life of Jesus. Here is "pneumatic" literature (as the Gnostic Valentinus called it). No one can decipher the meaning of John's message unassisted. This is literature meant to be understood only with the assistance of the Holy Spirit.

Smart Nicodemus comes to Jesus by night, cataloguing all the things he knows. In just a couple of moments with Jesus, this smart aleck is rendered into the freshman mumbling, "How can this be?" I don't know if Nicodemus became a believer and follower on the basis of this evening's conversation. Nicodemus is not mentioned again until the crucifixion of Jesus when Nicodemus asked the Sanhedrin for permission to give the body of Jesus a proper burial in Nicodemus's own tomb (making Nicodemus the patron saint of all morticians). I don't know for sure if Nicodemus asked for the dead body of Jesus as an act of piety or as a final, perverse attempt to shut Jesus up. John's Gospel adores ambiguity. I do know, in spite of all I don't know, that Jesus loves teasing thought in his parables and dislocating so-certain people through his parabolic gestures.

Nicodemus says that Jesus is "sent from God," a fancy biblical way of saying that Jesus is from elsewhere, outside of our experience, beyond our carefully trimmed worldview, unable easily to be grasped by our methods of knowledge. If you would think about Jesus, you must have a high tolerance for confusion. Throughout the Gospel of John, the typical, predominate response to Jesus from everybody who met him was, "How can this be?"

I used to stand in the pulpit of Duke Chapel, at the end of the grand Christmas Eve Service of Lessons and Carols, and read those sonorous King James Version cadences from the very first of the Gospel of John—"In the beginning was the Word, and the Word was with God. . . . In him was life; and the life was the light of men. And the light shineth in darkness; and the darkness comprehended it not."

Beautiful poetry, but what does that mean: "comprehended it not"?

I have spent more than forty years in advance study of Jesus. I can read those words in Greek, and I don't know for certain, to tell the truth, what they really, really mean.

I just know they're true. The truth is a person, personal, sometimes as confusing and unfathomable as any person may be, yet also as unavoidable and undeniable as the person seated next to me at dinner. Sorry, if you prefer your truth to come at you in absolute, definable form; Jesus Christ (a person who died violently and rose unexpectedly) is the way, the life, and the truth.

Supper with Satan

Satan enters the story of Jesus only once in John's Gospel, at 13:27. The title *devil* is used only three times (6:70;

8:44; and 13:2). All but one of these passages (8:44) refer to someone rejecting Christ. Twice Satan is called "the ruler of this world" in 12:31 and 14:30. The world that God loves enough to send the only son (3:16) is also a world under satanic presumptions to rule.

John says that Satan entered the heart of Judas, leading him to betrayal, even as he dipped his hand into the dish. But I remind you that all of the disciples were at table and that all fled into the darkness when the soldiers came to arrest Jesus. *All.*

John says the devil inspires Judas to betrayal (13:2). Earlier Judas was called a thief (12:6), but John does not ascribe Judas's betrayal to greed, saying that diabolical influence was the main motive.

Once again, John is leading us into deeper waters in which natural human actions occur against a backdrop of mysterious supernatural activity. We, who have been schooled to think of our actions as the sole activity within the world, may be challenged by John's notion that this world is also the product of a controversy by a loving God and a satanic adversary. As we are busy acting, other forces—other beings—may be acting upon us. Might it be that sometimes when I declare, "I have decided to...," what's really happening is, "I have been goaded into..."?

As a preacher, I'm tempted to tell the story of Judas's betrayal as a matter of betrayal by a friend. William Shakespeare worked this terrain so well before me. Betrayal by a friend is a fit subject for high drama. Just about anyone in the congregation readily empathizes with the events of this night as a human tragedy.

But John moves us into deeper waters than human-initiated betrayal and tragedy in which the great God of Love goes head-to-head with the Prince of Lies. John paints Judas's act as even more than a betrayal of a friend; it's a cosmic, divine struggle in which an ordinary person such as Judas has been commandeered by the forces of evil to play his bit part. More than mere greed was pushing Judas toward his act. John works that strange space between what is remembered of event and history and the theological significance of what is remembered, the world beyond mere history and mundane event.

Thus, a courtesy offered by Jesus with a basin and towel becomes an eternal claim upon the lives of his disciples. A betrayal by a friend becomes a decisive battle between God and Satan. Life here around the table becomes a window into life eternal. John's testimony is based upon actual historical events, but John aspires to be more than a mere historian; he is a storyteller attempting to draw us into the drama, a preacher wanting to speak us into a different world.

Great adventures and deep insights await the ones who dare to walk into the dark, boldly enter this world, and take their places as Jesus' table, even on a Thursday.

Notes

1. Timothy Williams, "Ex-Inmate Shares Stories of Stint as a Death Row Chef," *New York Times*, October 18, 2011. www.nytimes.com/2011/10/19

/us/former-inmate-shares-tricks-of-the-trade-of-a-death-row-chef
.html?pagewanted=all&_r=0.

2. Ibid.

3. Emily Dickinson, "The Blunder Is to Estimate," from *The Complete Poems of Emily Dickinson*, Faber and Faber, 1968, 23.

Why are we here at table with you, Jesus?

We're hungry.

Surely you know how difficult it is, in our culture of self-sufficiency, to publicly admit to our need.

Thanks for making us creatures who must acknowledge our emptiness, our fragility, our dependence three times a day. Thank you for reminding us that our hands were created for more than to grab, to reach, and to hold on tightly to what we have; our hands can also be open and grateful, receptive to the gift of food.

You know us. We think that we are on our own. We prefer fast food served instantly, at our demand. We like to eat on the run, while active and busy doing rather than passively receiving.

Thanks for teaching us dependency, patience, gratitude, and grace when you say, "All is ready. Come to the table." Amen.

CHAPTER V

BREAD FROM HEAVEN

"Very truly, I tell you, the one who believes in me will also do the works
that I do and, in fact, will do greater works than these, because I am
going to the Father. I will do whatever you ask in my name, so that
the Father may be glorified in the Son. If in my name you ask me for
anything, I will do it."
—John 14:12-14

E arlier Jesus proclaimed himself as the way, the truth, and the life. He is the singular, unique way for his followers to come to the Father. A few moments ago, at the table, Jesus told his disciples the truth, that one of them will betray him.

Jesus' talk of the truth makes all the more remarkable that Jesus makes two astounding claims for his followers: (1) they can do "greater works" than he has performed, and (2) if they ask for anything, he will do it.

Can Jesus be serious? We will do "greater works than these," greater works even than the works of the Son of God, the Light of the World? Note that Jesus promises that frail sinners such as we will do "greater works" "because [he is] going to the Father." That is, when followers do great things, they do so only through a relationship with Jesus who is in a unique relationship with God the Father. He is the vine; we are the branches. In Christ, God has done something about the problem between us and God. We who were so far off are invited to God's table, invited to be participants in God's great redemption of a lost world.

Thus Karl Barth said that when someone really hears revelation from God in Scripture, that is akin to God's creation of the world. It's a miracle on par with what God did in Genesis 1 or John 1, a whole new world. And when, in our little lives, we allow our lights to shine, when we dare play our bit part in the great drama of God's redemption of the world, it's something close to what Jesus has done for us dying sinners in his cross and resurrection. Thus Jesus makes the bold claim that our deeds will be even greater.

Jesus worked a great miracle in multiplying a few loaves and fishes to feed a multitude. A similar miracle is how Jesus is using people like you to multiply the good that he wants to do in the world.

Even before the dust began to settle after ninety tornadoes tore through Alabama in one day the week after Easter, I watched a church bus, full of volunteers of all ages, show up in a devastated little town. As people got off that bus, with tools in hand, to work with the victims of the storms, I saw the dawn of a whole new world, a light shining in the terrible dark.

As the conversation at the table moves in this direction, again Jesus is more than a great moral teacher, a stunning ethical example. He says that he is "going to the Father" so that "the Father may be glorified in the Son." In saying that we will do "greater works than these," Jesus implies that as he moves toward the Father, so do we. The Father is being glorified not only by the Son but also by sinners like us. Jesus is our way to God. As Jesus goes to the Father, he takes us along with him.

In a letter to one of his many troubled, turbulent congregations, Paul says that "God chose what is foolish" (us) in order to confound the wisdom of the world (1 Cor. 1:27). Paul there calls us refuse and garbage and says that we are miraculously redeemed by God to do God's work in the world.

It is as if God says, "Do you doubt that I am a glorious God? Then look at my handiwork in the lives of frail, fallen, finite creatures. Look at the church where that which the world considers 'of low degree' (that is, garbage) is made into something grand and glorious."

"If you love me, you will keep my commandments. And I will ask the Father, and he will give you another Advocate, to be with you forever. This is the Spirit of truth, whom the world cannot receive, because it neither sees him nor knows him. You know him, because he abides with you, and he will be in you."

—John 14:15-17

Friends

"I am the vine, and my Father is the vine-grower. He removes every branch in me that bears no fruit. Every branch that bears fruit he prunes to make it bear more fruit. You have already been cleansed by the word that I have spoken to you. Abide in me as I abide in you. Just as the branch cannot bear fruit by itself unless it abides in the vine, neither can you unless you abide in me. I am the vine, you are the branches. Those who abide in me and I in them bear much fruit, because apart from me you can do nothing. . . . I do not call you servants any longer, because the servant does not know what the master is doing; but I have called you friends, because I have made known to you every-thing that I have heard from my Father. You did not choose me but I chose you. And I appointed you to go and bear fruit, fruit that will last, so that the Father will give you whatever you ask him in my name. I am giving you these commands so that you may love one another."
—*John 15:1-5, 15-17*

"What a friend we have in Jesus," we sing, "all our sins and griefs to bear." Note that here at table Jesus doesn't say, "I'm your good friend," but rather he says, "I am calling you my good friends." He is making himself our friend, trans-forming us sinners and betrayers into his friends. Note that he tenderly calls us "friends" *after* he tells the truth about our collective betrayal. With friends like us, Jesus doesn't need enemies! A Christian is a sinner who, with the help of the Holy Spirit, responds in friendship to Jesus who has first befriended us. As Jesus reminds us, "You did not choose me but I chose you." Our being fruitful, faithful friends was Jesus' idea before it was ours.

When Jesus says, "I do not call you servants any lon-ger, . . . but I have called you friends, because I have made known to you everything that I have heard from my Father," at first this sounds warm and amicable. Who wouldn't rather be called someone's "friend" rather than "servant" (or more accurately in the Greek, "slave")?

Jesus seems to define his friendship as a matter of intimate revelation. He calls us friends because only a friend best knows the mind and heart of a friend. Jesus has loved us enough to hold nothing back but has "made known to you everything." Because in Christ, God Almighty has become our close friend, we need not stumble in the night, not knowing which way to turn. Jesus graciously tells us all we need to know to be in close fellowship with God. If Jesus hasn't told us something about God, we need not trouble ourselves about it.

Again, modern people often complain that if they knew more about God, if they had more information, then they could believe. Here at table, God is being defined, not as that distant being who stands above us in a great cloud of confusion, but rather as the friend who stands with us, telling us all we need to know to have eternal life—now.

When Jesus says that we are his beloved friends, let no one think that Jesus is letting us off lightly. You know that there is tough truth that can only be told to you by a friend. Also, there are things that you will do for a friend that you wouldn't do for anyone else. When you move from one apartment to another and ask for free help with the lifting, you will discover your true friends.

Transposing from the metaphor of friendship to that of

vine and branches, Jesus takes our relationship with him up to another level. Branches are organically connected to the vine. If they are disconnected from the vine, the branches die. When Jesus calls himself the "vine," he implies that we, the vine's branches, bear fruit not as lowly assistants or gofers but as full partners, fully connected to the Light of the World.

Loved in Order to Bear Fruit

Please note that the purpose of the branches is to "bear fruit." My church, judging from the numbers alone, has trouble with fruit these days. Part of me wishes that Jesus had said simply, "love me," or even, "love one another"; but no, talking to us with the severity and demand that only a friend can muster, he says that he expects us to bear fruit.

That next phrase, "so that the Father will give you whatever you ask him in my name" (John 5: 16), has raised questions from the church. I have heard that phrase used to bolster the alleged power of prayer. Whatever we ask, God will deliver, goes the reasoning.

Please note that the phrase "whatever you ask" is specifically related to lasting "fruit." Just as branches cannot bear fruit except as they are linked to the vine, so our fruitfulness is directly dependent upon our relatedness to Jesus.

This suggests to me that my own church would be better off if every four years at our General Conference, rather than meet and pass budgets and concoct more regulations, we prayed for fruit! Sadly, I fear that we doubt that Jesus is capable of fulfilling his promise to give us fruit if we "ask him in my name." Our lack of fruit may be due to a failure of faith.

I sent a pastor to a pitiful, moribund congregation in the eastern part of our conference. Upon her arrival, she told the congregation that one of her particular ministerial gifts was ministry with children, having earned her master's in early childhood education before attending seminary.

Their response? "We haven't had a children's Sunday school class in over a decade. No children."

When I visited the congregation a year later, I was thrilled to discover two children's ministry groups with a total of more than twenty children.

I asked the pastor, "What did you do to get these results?"

She replied, "I prayed. I told the Lord, 'If you want this church to have a future, you'll have to do it. Please, Lord, send us some of your kids so they can be our kids, and we promise to do the rest.' In only six months of continuous prayer, we got our first young family."

The Lord had made good on his promise: "the Father will give you whatever [fruit] you ask him in my name."

I also had a church that was in serious decline primarily due to constant congregational conflict. "For a long time we have prayed to God to heal our divisions," the pastor said, "to give us peace and harmony as a church."

Though I didn't think of John 15 at the time, I ought to have replied, "Don't pray for healing and harmony. Pray for God to make good on the promise for fruit. If you bear fruit, the healing and harmony will take care of themselves."

Jesus as Bread

Did the Twelve, gathered with Jesus for that last supper, think back on prior meals with Jesus? John 6 is one of the most revelatory chapters in the Gospel of John, divided among Jesus' feeding of the crowd (vv. 1-15), his walk on the water (vv. 16-21), and then an exchange between Jesus and the crowd after the feeding. Food for the multitude is a "sign" (*semeon*), a wondrous act that reveals who Jesus is. Dating this sign near the Passover (6:4) may be a linkage with the Last Supper, or it may be mere chronology. Of course, few things are "merely" anything in this Gospel.

A large crowd kept following him, because they saw the signs that he was doing for the sick.... Now the Passover...was near.... Then Jesus took the loaves, and when he had given thanks, he distributed them to those who were seated; so also the fish, as much as they wanted.... When the people saw the sign that he had done, they began to say, "This is indeed the prophet who is to come into the world."

When Jesus realized that they were about to come and take him by force to make him king, he withdrew again to the mountain by himself.

When evening came, his disciples went down to the lake, got into a boat, and started across the lake.... It was now dark.... The lake became rough because a strong wind was blowing.... They saw Jesus walking on the lake and coming near the boat, and they were terrified. But he said to them, "It is I; do not be afraid."

Jesus said to them, "I am the bread of life. Whoever comes to me will never be hungry."
—John 6:2, 4, 11, 14-16, 18-20, 35

It is common to lament that we lack enough knowledge of God to say anything definitive about God. Yet sometimes God is too much, at least according to John. In John 2, when the wine runs out at the bash after the wedding, Jesus doesn't just turn water into wine; he turns out 180 gallons of wine. (I'm a Methodist, so I don't personally know much about alcohol, but isn't that too much wine?)

Now a few chapters later there is a similar story of abundance, told not in wine but in bread. The story begins with mention of mountain, sea, and Passover. Get it? This may be some sort of redoing of Moses's liberation of Israel. Are the five barley loaves a hint of the five books of Moses? Anytime Jesus shows up, things mean more than they first appear. At Passover, the lambs are slaughtered; at this Passover, we shall witness the sacrifice of "the Lamb of God who takes away the sin of the world" (John 1:29). The metaphorical feast that John sets before us is almost too rich for consumption.

A little boy is enlisted, his gifts taken and used for the miraculous distribution. Here I'll suppress my homiletical urge to work this little boy's contribution up into a full-blown discourse on the way that Jesus loves to work with those whom the world regards as insignificant and with the small. But feel free to preach that sermon to yourself.

Jesus takes bread, gives thanks (*eucharisteo*), and shares, actions that you have witnessed in your church every time your church celebrates the Lord's Supper. An anticipation of Christian Eucharist? Maybe. Because this meal for the multitudes is at the center of John's Gospel, we wonder. For John, inciting wonderment in us is enough; belabored explanations await later preachers like me.

The disciples gather up twelve baskets (for the twelve tribes of Israel?) of leftovers, even as the children of Israel before them gathered manna in the wilderness. There is not just enough bread; there is more than enough. Jesus doesn't just have compassion on the hungry multitude; his love overflows. Surely this was one of our problems with Jesus—he was more God than we could handle. We attempt to explain him, to handle him with our human modes of explication, to confine him within our accustomed categories, and still there is a surplus of meaning. Our thirst could have been assuaged by water; he gives us 180 gallons of wine. We could have made it through the night with a couple of slices of bread; he gives enough bread and then some.

Note that Jesus enlists his disciples to work with him, using them to accomplish his mission. In distributing and in gathering up the loaves, the disciples are imitating him, even as he commands them to imitate him at a later meal when he stoops down and washes their feet. In following Jesus, the line between adoringly worshiping Jesus and ethically imitating Jesus is meant to be thin.

I know a couple of older women who take a few dozen chocolate chip cookies out to the county jail, hand them to people incarcerated there, and watch as those cookies are miraculously transformed into an overflowing of God's love and life even in that house of hate and death.

John 6:15 shows that the multitudes misunderstand Jesus, even as his disciples would misunderstand him at his last supper. We confuse physical hungers with spiritual ones. Having been miraculously fed, we seek to enthrone the wonder-worker as a religious celebrity, leading Jesus to flee us. Can Jesus have even greater things in store for us than the miraculous production of bread?

Although we are knee-deep in miraculous signs, the One "from above" graciously uses our gifts here below—a little boy's gift of loaves and fishes, and our gifts too.

Living Bread

The next thing you know, Jesus walks on water (John 6:16-21). It is the Gospel of John, after all. Which sign is more wondrous: feeding hungry people or walking on water? Unlike the Synoptic accounts of Jesus walking on water, the disciples here are not brought to faith (Matt. 14:33), but neither are they confused and clueless (Mark 6:51-52). The disciples simply welcome Jesus after his stroll across the sea. Take that as a metaphor for being encountered by Jesus in John. We don't have to devise a well-thought-out system of belief in Jesus, nor must we get our heads clear about him. We are to welcome him, welcoming him in all his paradoxical otherness and his threatening closeness.

The next section is our main concern: a pericope that is often called the "Bread of Life Discourse" (John 6:22-71). At first reading, this long, meandering monologue seems to cry out for a concise editor. I urge you to hear it as an anthem, a praise song in which beloved exclamations of faith are repeated, piled one upon another, and sung to highest heaven rather than argued or explained.

Jesus promises "food that endures for eternal life" (v. 27). Then there's a request from the crowd for a reassuring "sign" and their remembrance of Moses's miraculous feeding of manna to the people in the wilderness (vv. 30-31). There was no easy correlation between the gift of manna in the wilderness and the Israelites' trust in God, nor will Jesus play into our desire for easy, knock-down arguments for belief in him. Signs and wonders, as welcomed as they may be by us, are ambiguous at best and sometimes downright misleading.

Jesus reminds the crowd that God and not Moses fed people, playing on the manna theme and talking about bread that "comes down from heaven," prompting the people to request that sort of "wonder" bread (vv. 32-34). Bread is a good thing, but even as (in the other Gospels) Jesus refuses to turn stones to bread (Matt. 4:3), again we are reminded that Jesus is about something even more significant than feeding hungry people. Jesus says, "I am the living bread that came down from heaven" (John 6:51).

Our earnest prayer is: "Give us this bread always" (6:34).

Here I confess that as a preacher I'm often guilty of presenting the good news of Jesus Christ as if Jesus is mainly about giving us bread. Too many of my sermons say, in effect, "Are you looking for some deeper meaning in life?" Jesus can produce that for you. "Are you looking for a purpose-driven existence?" Jesus can come up with that too. "Need a reason to get out of bed in the morning," or "Looking for greater peace in your life?" Jesus delivers.

See? The gospel is thereby presented as a solution to our human problems, as we define our problems. I recently passed a highway billboard on which a smiling preacher, clutching a large Bible, says, "The Bible is the answer to every one of your problems."

Makes me wonder if that pastor has ever actually read the Bible.

I've found the Bible to be the solution to some of my problems, yet I can also testify that the Savior attested to in scripture is also the onset of problems I never had before I met Jesus! Scripture is not here to meet my needs. I live in a culture that tends to produce people who are bundles of omnivorous need, a culture in which few people are given the insight to know which desires are worth having. Scripture is divine; that is, it is produced by some need that God has to speak to and to reveal God's self to us. And surely John would want us to say that encounters with God, at least the Word Made Flesh, often leave us with more questions than answers.

Anyone who, like the crowds in John 6, hankers after

Jesus, hoping for bread to fill the stomach, will eventually be disappointed. Jesus has compassion on hungry, hurting people. But he is about even more than that. Jesus is not the means whereby we get from God whatever our hearts desire; Jesus is God's means of getting out of us what God desires.

If I sound as if I'm making following the Word Made Flesh too daunting a task, surely John would have me to remind you that no one is supposed to follow Jesus alone. Jesus gives us the "Paraclete" (John 14:16, "Advocate" in NRSV), the Holy Spirit who tells us things we can't tell ourselves and who enables us to do those things we could never do on our own.

All of this takes place in an earthly, mundane context, but we will require external assistance from that mysterious presence, the Paraclete, who "will teach you everything, and remind you of all that I [Jesus] have said to you" (14:26), someone who will "guide you into all the truth" (16:13). The good news is that we are not "orphaned" (14:18). We are the recipients of pneumatic help. The one who "abides with you...will be in you" (14:17), giving us all we need to know in order to follow Jesus and to bear fruit.

"I still have many things to say to you, but you cannot bear them now. When the Spirit of truth comes, he will guide you into all the truth; for he will not speak...to you the things that are to come. He will glorify me, because he will take what is mine and declare it to you."
—John 16:12-14

In many of our minds, the Holy Spirit is a comfort-bringer and a caregiver who soothes our hearts. In John's

Gospel, the Paraclete, the Holy Spirit, is known mostly as a teacher and guide. We couldn't take the full force of Christ's truth at the table or in the days that he walked with us on earth. So the Son returns to the Father and sends to us a Teacher who will "guide you into all truth." Thank goodness that God does not expect people like us to be faithful or loving on our own. We are given not only the great command to love but also the means.

One of the Holy Spirit's appointed means is the Gospel of John, this curious mix of the earthly and the heavenly, whereby we begin with a story about hungry people being satisfied with wonder bread only to end the story with Jesus flat-out saying, "*I* am bread, bread from heaven, come down to your level." Thus our eyes are opened, and we see dimensions of something as quotidian and common as bread as nothing less than the near presence of God with Us. John gradually—strange story followed by weird comment—leads us to believe. Something's afoot.

At this point I'm not too troubled if you fear that the water is getting too deep for you. I have faith that Jesus will reveal to you what he wants you to see of his love for you. When he leads you forth on some strange spiritual sea, remember, he won't leave you orphaned, nor will he send you away empty. He will continue to surprise you, to show up to you, to feed you bread you couldn't earn, to lead you to cry out, "Give us *this* bread always" (6:34, italics mine).

By my experienced estimate, two out of four of us show up at church on Sunday for the wrong reasons. We are there looking for what we think we've just got to have—inner peace, meaning in life, answers to all our questions, bread—more than we want God. But Jesus doesn't leave us to our wrong reasons and our self-centered stratagems. He keeps working with us, feeding us, opening our eyes, transforming us, sometimes not giving us what we want, but giving us what he knows, in his love, we need. We keep misunderstanding him, keep being confused by him. He says *bread*, and immediately we begin to salivate and our stomachs start to grumble.

Then the Word Made Flesh comes to us, works with us; and before we know it, what we thought we wanted no longer makes much sense, and we cry out, as multitudes have before us, "Give us this bread always" (6:34).

Eating and Drinking Jesus

The Jews then disputed among themselves, saying, "How can this man give us his flesh to eat?" So Jesus said to them, "Very truly, I tell you, unless you eat the flesh of the Son of Man and drink his blood, you have no life in you. Those who eat my flesh and drink my blood have eternal life, and I will raise them up on the last day; for my flesh is true food and my blood is true drink. Those who eat my flesh and drink my blood abide in me, and I in them. Just as the living Father sent me, and I live because of the Father, so whoever eats me will live because of me. This is the bread that came down from heaven. . . . The one who eats this bread will live forever."

—John 6:52-58

The third part of the Bread Discourse of chapter 6 (vv. 52-59) contains some of the most disputed verses in John. The existential biblical critic Rudolf Bultmann argued that these verses were the work of a later "ecclesiastical redactor" who added the verses in order to make this Gospel more "sacramental" and therefore more palatable to the established church.[1] I fear that Bultmann's Protestant prejudices got the best of him. Historical critics have this tendency to treat a Gospel as if it were a hostile witness in the dock, forced to explain why the Gospel's witness is truth rather than fanciful fabrication.

Do these verses—with their talk of drinking Jesus' blood and eating his body—refer to the Eucharist? I don't know. (Hey, it's the Gospel of John!) I do know that some of the earliest commentators immediately thought they did. These preachers quite justifiably thought "Lord's Supper" when they heard Jesus talk about bread and wine, body and blood. In fact, as the Lord's Supper fell into disuse in some Protestant churches, I wonder if we lost the means to think in a way that was sacramentally suitable for thinking with the Gospel of John.

I would be so bold as to say that scripture such as John 6:52-59 ought always to be read in the context of the Lord's Supper (the normal context for all scripture, I remind you). To do so would make the question, "Is Jesus referring to himself in these verses or to the elements of the Lord's Supper?" a false dichotomy. Jesus has repeatedly called himself "bread." Now he is the "living bread" (v. 51), which bread is "my flesh" ("flesh" is the same Greek word, *sarx,* as in John 1:14).

Talk of drinking blood and eating flesh is more than the

opponents of Jesus can take. Jesus' words are even more offensive in the Greek in which "eat" (*phagein*) in verses 51-53 becomes "gnaw" or "gobble up" (*trogo*), the same way that animals desperately gobble their food.

Wow. Are you able to go this far with the Incarnation? Wouldn't it have been easier if Jesus had said, "Think about me," or "Feel emotional about me"? No. He says, "Eat my flesh; drink my blood." In other words, Jesus says that we must go after him the way a dog goes for meat, the way the Cookie Monster handles cookies, the way...well, you get my drift.

Sorry, if you like your saviors to be rational, urbane, and coolly detached, someone who resembles the wandering wisdom teacher, the Jesus Seminar's Jesus. Once again, Jesus gets physical and intimate. He will not allow us to deal with him the way we usually deal with other people—allowing them to come close, but only so close. Jesus is God up close and personal.

Thomas Merton said that in our culture to say that "God is love" has as little impact as to say one should "eat Wheaties." Sentimentality (a worse sin among us even than atheism) takes an otherwise good idea such as "God is love" and perverts it into something vague and innocuous. Sentimentality, said Flannery O'Connor, is the religious equivalent of pornography. We have a vague, pleasurable experience of something without having to invest or to risk transformation.

Thus we are challenged by the Gospel of John's presentation of "love." God's love for us in Christ is more than thought or feeling; it is nothing less than a physical, total ingestion of God, taking God into the core of our being, imbibing God the way I saw a starving little boy in Haiti take down a bowl of life-giving rice and beans.

To all those who think that "religion" is "what you do with your solitude" (Schleiermacher) or "a purpose-driven life" (Rick Warren) or "the Be-Happy-Attitudes" (Robert Schuller) or even the ethically noble "Do unto others as you would have them do unto you," Jesus takes things up more than a notch or two. Sorry, if you think Jesus wants your soul; he wants all of you, including your gastrointestinal tract. Pity, if you presumed that God wanted only an hour or so of your time for the Lord's Supper; God wants to be with you every single meal, including snacks, inhabiting the very core of your being.

No wonder that many in the clutching crowd ceased trooping after Jesus after he made these statements (John 6:53-59). Even some of the disciples whined, "This is a hard saying!" It's off-putting to our sense of spiritual decorum to be encountered by a God who crudely demands, "Eat my flesh; drink my blood."

Watching those who were previously attracted to Jesus— when he handed out free bread or spoke on antique biblical themes such as manna—walk away when Jesus made the spiritual too close for comfort, Jesus asks his disciples, "Will you also go away?"

The Twelve spoke for all of us, including those of you who at this point may be put off by some of the material in this book about Jesus: "Lord, where can we go? You have the words of eternal life."

Time and again we have tried more congenial gods, have attempted easier self-help techniques. Now, having come to the end of our efforts at self-salvation and god-construction, we have nowhere to turn except toward the One who speaks "words of eternal life."

In *Il Purgatorio*, Virgil—who embodies the best wisdom from the classical tradition—guides Dante through the various levels of the afterlife. Toward the end of *Purgatorio*, Virgil expounds upon the way that leads to life, giving Dante his last words of wisdom in much the same way as Jesus spoke his last words at the supper. But Virgil's words sound confused and conflicted, without much wisdom or direction. I think this is Dante's way of saying that even the classical wisdom of Plato or Aristotle can take one only so far.

Virgil counsels Dante to seek the middle way, the way of temperance and reasonable balance. Lacking the specifically Christian virtues—faith, hope, and (above all) love—Virgil, being a classical man, advocates moderation, less intense passion, not more. As a Christian, Dante compares his erotic passion for Beatrice to his devotion to Christ. The way forward is more-intense love, even-more-passionate engagement, not less. The challenge is not the classical moderation in all things but rather more-passionate love for a more appropriate object.

Dante dares to make his romantic passion for Beatrice the most appropriate way to think about the Christian life. (This is why, I think, Dante is gentle with the sins of sexual passion, placing those guilty of sexual sin toward the top of purgatory, rather than on the bottom. They are guilty of misplaced passion rather than truly rebellious sin.) As a Christian, Dante knows that wholehearted engagement with the object of one's love is good. Our human engagement with Christ places us in the orbit of the eternal love that moves the sun, the moon, and the stars.

Friends and foes said many things about Jesus. I can't recall anyone accusing him of being "balanced," "dispassionate," or "moderate."

Mother Teresa, a visible embodiment of Christ's love, was a fanatic. So was Martin Luther King Jr. Thank God these modern saints did not, in moderation, turn away from the risky, totally involving love that voraciously feeds upon the Bread of Life and produces the good fruit that is entailed by life on the vine.

To the End, He Abides with Us

"I am the true vine, and my Father is the vinegrower. He removes every branch in me that bears no fruit. Every branch that bears fruit he prunes to make it bear more fruit. You have already been cleansed by the word that I have spoken to you. Abide in me as I abide in you. Just as the branch cannot bear fruit by itself unless it abides in the

vine, neither can you unless you abide in me. I am the vine, you are the branches. Those who abide in me and I in them bear much fruit."
—John 15:1-5

The first thing that impressed the believers on the first Easter was absence. As he had predicted at the table, Jesus had gone away. A couple of disciples ran out to the tomb and peered in, and it was, alas, empty. They assumed, quite rationally, that in one final indignity, someone had stolen the body of Jesus. So they sigh deeply, give up, and go back home (John 20:1-18).

Mary, in her grief, lingers. In the darkness, someone appears. Mary assumes he is a gardener and says, "Sir, they've taken away my Lord and I don't know where to find him."

The gardener calls her by name, "Mary," and she says, in her startled recognition, "My Lord."

"Abide with me, fast the evening falls," we sing in the beloved hymn. "Stay with me," we plead; night is falling, and we know the peril of being alone in the dark. The hymn is an allusion to the story of the supper at Emmaus when a couple of disciples, startled that Jesus "had been made known to them in the breaking of the bread," pleaded with the risen Christ, "stay with us" (Luke 24: 29, 35).

Interestingly, in John 15, while promising to abide with us, Jesus spends most of his table talk urging us to abide with him. It's as if Jesus says that his abiding with us is not the problem; the great challenge is our ability to abide with him.

Our spirits are as fickle as the wind. We burn hot, fully committed, one moment, coolly drifting the next. How can Jesus expect vacillators like us to be consistent in our friendship? Right after Jesus' talk about "abiding," Peter, the premier disciple, will betray his Lord when the going gets rough.

How can Jesus expect people like us to abide in him? I think Jesus is able to command us to abide in him because of his sure and certain promise to abide in us, never to let us go. Elsewhere (in Matt. 18:20), Jesus promised that if even two or three of us gather (at the table?), he will join us for the food and fellowship.

Our story with God does not end at the cross on Friday, as we expected. Jesus told us that eventually we would understand. There, on the beach, we got his point—it isn't over between us and God until God says it's over. The Last Supper wasn't really the last supper; it was the beginning, not the end, of table time with Jesus. The risen Christ shows up, transforming our painful, tragic absence by his presence. In steadfast love, God refuses to leave us. Christ shows up and appears to the very ones who betrayed and disappointed him. We don't have to go looking for Jesus; he's always looking for us. We don't have to search and find him; he finds us.

My favorite theologian, Karl Barth, once quipped, "Christians go to church to make their last stand against God."

Guilty. Sometimes the dignity, order, beauty, and spiritual fuzz of church are perverse defense against a death-defying

God. The purpose of church—to meet and to be met by God—can be abused as a means of avoiding God.

Still, countless times I've seen people flee inside a seemingly safe, secluded sanctuary only to be smacked upside the head, jumped by the God whom they had relegated to heaven.

I recall the student who muttered on his exit one Sunday after we had celebrated the Lord's Supper in Duke Chapel, "So? It really is true, after all?" I took him as a victim of the divine dragnet of grace. Once again, the Paraclete had pounced upon a seemingly harmless endeavor like the sharing of bread and wine, using it as a means of entrapment. Perhaps that student thought he had come away for a polite academic discussion of God, which is sometimes attempted in the Department of Religion, only to get jumped by a real God who loves surprise.

I recall a visitor who exited, not with the usual, annoying, "Isn't the choir just wonderful?" but rather with, "I just met the God I've spent my life avoiding." Gotcha.

Israel had a tabernacle—portable "tent of meeting" housing the ark with tablets of Moses. I remind you that John's Gospel begins not only with "the Word became flesh" (which would be miracle enough) but also with the even more astounding "and the Word" (*eskenosen in hemin*) and "the Word tented among us"—the miracle of the Incarnation. Church is really church whenever, wherever God uses our human rituals to make a divine tent of meeting.

So, I leave you with a concluding meal in the Gospel of

John (21:1-19). As things turned out for the Eleven, the "last supper" wasn't really the last. Our story with God, by God's grace, continues. After the crucifixion, the disciples return to what they did before Jesus called them and so disrupted their lives—they're fishing. The response of Jesus' disciples to his cruel cross and astounding resurrection? Disbelief, doubt, and a relentless determination to get back their world before Jesus.

"It was a good campaign while it lasted, even though we didn't get him elected Messiah. The road trips were fun, but the preaching, healing, and exorcisms were often a drag. Let's go fishing."

"We ought to get together sometime and remember the good old days on the road," one chirped.

"Yeah, like a sort of memorial meal for veterans of the Jesus Campaign," said another.

Ah, back to the reassuring, anesthetizing calm of the normal! (Sometimes our yearning for Monday is a means of escaping the oddness of Sunday.) At last we can get over the weirdness of the world within the Gospel of John and get back to the comfortable, quotidian life before Jesus. They resume what they were doing before Jesus appeared among them as Word Made Flesh and disrupted them. They are fishing, a most prosaic, routine, and regimented way to make a living.

Unfortunately for the disciples' yearning for a world made safe from God, it's the Gospel of John, and there are surprises everywhere, whether it's friends about a supper table on Thursday or fellow fisherfolk having breakfast on a beach on Monday.

A stranger calls out from the beach, "Kids, caught any fish?"

Those who weren't good at discipling are not much better at fishing. The stranger gives expert fishing advice, then kindles a fire for breakfast. Peter is the first to figure out that the stranger is none other than Jesus. He's back. Jesus, true to form, has returned to the same group of losers who so disappointed him in the first place. He is back, doing what he did before: inviting them to table, taking, breaking, giving food. Communion.

The risen Christ doesn't just come back, but as usual he enlists, summons, instructs, and commands them: "love me and feed my lambs." He repeats the command to love three times. (He's worked with these knuckleheads before.) Peter, who denied Jesus three times (John 18:15-18), now thrice declares his love for Jesus.

On the beach, Monday morning, is a reunion—an unsought, unexpected, maybe even unwanted reunion. Experience of the presence of a living God is not something postponed until some distant eternity. Eternity is now. The same Jesus whom we knew at the table is with us in the power of the Holy Spirit here and now. We are not orphans; he abides with us.

See? It wasn't just that Jesus was raised from the dead; it

was that he immediately engaged in communion. He came back to those who had failed him and, all evidence to the contrary, once again ordains them to be about his work: "Love, as I loved you. Do the same things I've done to you."

The Bible may be read as a book of constant communion and reiterated reunion—for example, Abraham and Sarah meet God on a starry night, Jacob is wrestled to the ground beside the River Jabbok, Mary is hailed by an angel, and the disciples are found on the beach by the Jesus they thought they had lost.

To be honest, sometimes we want communion; sometimes we don't. Sometimes those who know Jesus best—such as church people, for instance—knowing firsthand how demanding a present Jesus, as opposed to an absent Jesus, can be, are the most likely to attempt to avoid Jesus. And sometimes those who don't know Jesus—such as un-churched people, for instance—frequently miss Jesus when he unexpectedly shows up to them.

But one point of this Easter story of breakfast on the beach is: it's not up to us anyway. Tabernacle, meeting, and communion are things that Jesus does. I think John believes that whether you have prayed to the risen Christ to come into your life or not, he will. As you share food and fellowship with friends at supper, or fix some fish on the beach, keep looking over your shoulder. The risen Christ will jump at almost any opportunity to reveal himself to you.

So maybe I should not have subtitled this book,

Encountering Jesus at the Lord's Table as if for the Last Time, but should have put it more in the spirit of John's Gospel—*Encountered by Jesus at the Lord's Table*. Note that we don't speak of risen Christ "sightings," as if we were perceptive enough to see Jesus. It's resurrection "appearances"—revelation is always in God's hands, God self-revealing, and God showing up in God's own good time. And Christians have discovered, down through the ages, that God most often shows up when we're at the table, just having a meal, with just a few close or difficult friends, only to exclaim with Jacob before us, "Surely the LORD is in this place—and I did not know it!" (Gen. 28:16).

What is your great hope in life, in death, and in life beyond death? The same persistent Savior who shows up to Mary shall, in your living and your dying, often when you least expect him, keep showing up to you.

I know someone who wants so very much to believe but, as yet, just can't. I told her to relax. Though she, as yet, does not have faith in Christ, I have faith that Christ will give her the gift that he has graciously given so many of us—Christ will show up.

After many years as a campus pastor—giving unsolicited advice to students and exploring whether they think they are or are not Christian, how little they can believe about Jesus and still make it under the bar, and how good they have to be and still be considered a member of the flock—I finally came to a simple definition of Christianity (and you know how academics hate simple definitions): *A Christian is anybody who has been encountered by Jesus. A recipient of reunion.*

Communion is good news for some. Relax, Christianity is not what you think or feel about Jesus—it's what Jesus does to you. It's not a technique for how you use him, but it's how he uses you.

Here's the bad news for others: your attempts to escape are futile. If Jesus means to show up to you in church or at breakfast on the beach or in the kitchen, give in, give up, say yes, and relent to communion.

There are lots of reasons why people don't attend church regularly—boring sermons, amateur musicians, a surplus of people my age—the list is endless. Most of us who work regularly with Jesus know another reason why people aren't in church—*Jesus!* When Jesus shows up, even at suppertime, he thinks nothing of making large, outrageous demands upon his best friends, like loving his other friends.

I remember a conversation in which I lamented the relatively small number of students we attracted to Duke Chapel. A student responded, "Go easy on yourself. I've heard you preach. It's amazing that you get anybody. Look. Duke attracts people who are smart enough to know that if Jesus showed up, their lives would become more difficult than they already are. No wonder they sleep in."

Jesus, the one whom we tried to push out of our world on a cross, shall reign, shall gather every living creature to himself, calling us to the table, living reunited with the dead, the lost, found, and everybody, in the end...home.

At the Last Supper, when Jesus knelt down and washed our feet, he said he was preparing to go back to his Father, stopping awhile to prepare his disciples for the future. What does the future hold for us? Where are we headed? Who wins the great, cosmic struggle between God and Satan?

At the last table in Jerusalem, Jesus prepares us for the next table in your church, and for that great table in eternity. He gives us a glimpse, not only of the cross that lies ahead, but also of his, and our, destiny. His love for us is eternal. He who urges us to abide in him, promises to abide with us. In the end, as we join at the great feast on high, we shall then know: we're not fated for separation, loneliness, exile, or autonomy in the cold, dark, uncaring cosmos. We were made for meeting. Creation is always being coaxed to communion. We shall be raised for reunion.

You don't believe it? Here, have some wine, and take some bread.

Notes

1. My friend D. Moody Smith raised good questions about Bultmann's thesis on chapter 6 in his seminal work, *The Composition and Order of the Fourth Gospel* (New Haven: Yale University Press, 1965). Moody is our grandest contemporary interpreter of John's Gospel.